ST. LOUIS TRAILBLAZER
ERMA BERGMANN

FROM PITCHER'S MOUND TO PATROL

PATRICIA TREACY

Foreword by
Hall of Famer Ozzie Smith

THE
History
PRESS

Published by The History Press
Charleston, SC
www.historypress.com

Front cover, top left: courtesy Erma Bergmann; *top center*: courtesy Gene Donaldson; *top right*: courtesy Erma Bergmann; *bottom*: courtesy Erma Bergmann.
Back cover, top: courtesy St. Louis Police Department Library; *center*: courtesy Erma Bergmann; *bottom*: courtesy Erma Bergmann.

First published 2023

Manufactured in the United States

ISBN 9781467155373

Library of Congress Control Number: 2023940767

CONTENTS

FOREWORD

I first met Erma at the Missouri History Museum in Forest Park in 2004, when *Baseball as America* came to St. Louis. This was a traveling exhibit from Cooperstown. Our paths crossed again at various baseball shows. I was quickly taken by Erma's warmth and friendliness. She's probably never met anyone she didn't like. There are no strangers to Erma, just people she's waiting to meet.

When Erma was recruited to try out for the All-American Girls Professional Baseball League in 1945, she never could have imagined that one day she'd be in the Hall of Fame. The 1940s was a different age for women. They wore aprons, not baseball uniforms. They walked around in high heels, not spikes.

But here were these daring women playing fiercely competitive baseball, entertaining fans across the Midwest and taking up the slack created by Major League Baseball players who were serving their country during World War II.

All the players in the women's league were inducted into Cooperstown in 1988. This turned out to be one of four Halls of Fame Erma joined.

She played outfield and third base in the St. Louis Amateur Softball League from 1938 to 1945 and entered its Hall of Fame in 1996.

When Erma was nominated for the Missouri Sports Hall of Fame, I wrote a letter recommending her. I drove to Springfield and attended her induction dinner in 2007. I was proud to see her sitting at the elevated head table, the only woman in that year's class of fifteen inductees. Even though

Erma Bergmann and Ozzie Smith, St. Louis Cardinals Hall of Famer. *Courtesy Gene Donaldson.*

she was in her eighties, her voice was strong and without hesitation as she thanked all those who were there and those who were not there.

Matt Blunt, the governor of Missouri at the time, sent her a proclamation. St. Louis was proud of Erma, too. Mayor Francis Slay declared February 11, 2007, "Erma M. Bergmann Day in St. Louis." She became part of the St. Louis Sports Hall of Fame in 2011.

After Erma hung up her spikes and left the ball field, she joined the St. Louis Metropolitan Police Department. She served the citizens of St. Louis as a policewoman for twenty-five years.

Erma is a model citizen and an ambassador for baseball. She's a role model for women, young adults and children alike.

When Ballpark Village opened in St. Louis, Erma was surprised to see her signed baseball contract from 1947 along with a baseball she autographed many years ago included in the museum.

Erma has followed her passions throughout her life, first as an excellent professional woman's baseball player and then as a dedicated policewoman. When you're willing and able to follow your passions like Erma has, you never really "work" a day in your life.

Erma lived a rich and rewarding life.

—Ozzie Smith
Summer 2014

PREFACE

ST. LOUIS TRAILBLAZER

Erma Bergmann sat in a field box at Busch Stadium, compliments of the St. Louis Cardinals, celebrating her eighty-fourth birthday. It was early June 2008.

The curls of her white hair blew in the breeze. Her porcelain skin was almost transparent. Her smooth hands were those of a woman several decades younger, a fine lady who had never dipped her hands in a scrub bucket or wrapped her fingers around a baseball.

Erma munched nachos and hot peppers, sipped a Bud Light and reminisced about her life.

In 1945, at age twenty-one, she was recruited to play with the All-American Girls Professional Baseball League. She signed a contract for seventy-five dollars a week and became a pitcher. She fired a no-hitter on May 22, 1947, and recorded an earned run average of 1.74 that year.

When Erma stepped off the pitcher's mound for the last time in 1954, she embraced a new challenge as a policewoman in the St. Louis Metropolitan Police Department. Erma served in the Juvenile Division and in the Decoy, Rape and Hoodlum Squads during her twenty-five-year career with the department.

As an octogenarian, honors rained down like fly balls dropping in the outfield. She's in four Halls of Fame, including at Cooperstown, New York.

I met Erma in 2005 through a friend from whom she had bought a camera. During the transaction, Erma mentioned her careers. She thought somebody should write a book about her, and they called me. Erma and

I later sat down across her kitchen table, and she told me about her life. I quickly realized that this was living history that should be shared.

"When we're all gone, who will there be to tell it like it was?" Erma questioned me.

Erma and I began a long friendship. Interviews with her colleagues from baseball and the police department revealed a woman of courage and strength. She was a pioneer in sports and law enforcement, and her life is intriguing and inspiring.

—Patricia Treacy
July 15, 2020

LETTER FROM ERMA BERGMANN

Dear Friends,

I grew up during the Great Depression. In my wildest dreams, I never imagined the exciting life that was ahead. Playing ball opened a whole new world for me.

How would I know that a movie, A League of Their Own, *would spark interest in us old gals who played baseball during World War II? I never thought I'd be answering fan mail from around the world some sixty years after I fired my last pitch.*

I spent twenty-five years as a policewoman. There were some hair-raising experiences, especially when I served on the Decoy Squad. I'm often asked, "Were you scared? Of course I was scared. You'd have to be off your rocker if you weren't afraid."

Through the years, people told me, "Someone should write a book about your life." My story is my legacy. My life proves that things can be accomplished, wherever or whenever, if you have a gift or a talent plus perseverance. My accomplishments weren't ordinary, but they were attainable.

While Pat was gathering information for the book, she arranged get-togethers with some of my old friends and teammates. We had lunch with Mayme Raines, one of my old softball pals. Mayme died about a month later. I was glad we got to see each other again.

It was a great feeling for me to reminisce with good friends from so long ago. You wonder where "so long ago" went! This is where history comes from.

My life is part of American history. I hope you enjoy reading about it.

Erma M. Bergmann

ACKNOWLEDGEMENTS

Just like the game of baseball, this book is a team effort. My sincere thanks to the following:

Millie and Sharon Costello introduced me to Erma. Without them, this book would never have been written. Millie also suggested that the book include a letter from Erma to her readers. Since Erma passed away before her book was published, this suggestion was invaluable.

Tim Morrison handled the technical difficulties that plagued this project. When the manuscript was swallowed up in my computer, Tim rescued it. Helen Muser deciphered the editing symbols that appeared when the document was resurrected.

Melba Krebs Buxbaum, PhD, and Grady Smith, fellow writers and high school classmates, edited the manuscript.

Gene Donaldson, a friend, traveled to Springfield, Missouri, and photographed Erma when she was inducted into the Missouri Sports Hall of Fame. Julie Kurz and the late Audrey Kissel Lafser, Erma's best friends, contributed many tidbits of Erma's life.

My thanks to the All-American Girls Professional Baseball League Players Association, especially Merrie Fidler, whose book *The Origins and History of the AAGPBL* was an excellent resource. Rick Chapman, whose mother was Erma's catcher, granted permission to use the picture of Erma's baseball card in the book. He is the president of the Players Association.

My thanks goes to former players Sister Toni Palermo, Dolly White and Lefty Alvarez and many other players and associate members who were interviewed. I offer my gratitude to members of the St. Louis Metropolitan Police Department who worked with Erma and passed their memories on to me. Thanks, too, to Barbara Miksicek, retired head of the St. Louis Police Library.

Thanks, too, to my friends who continued to encourage the completion of this book.

1

A COLORFUL FAMILY

My pop apprenticed as a packinghouse butcher in Germany for two years. He worked for free, receiving room and board and a glass of beer at bedtime. Can you imagine someone today working for nothing?
—Erma Bergmann

Erma Bergmann's roots were sunk in German soil. Her father was born in 1886 in Schirradorf, Germany, a town of about 250 people near Nuremberg. Otto Bergmann was the seventh of nine sons, enough boys for a baseball team.

Otto von Bismarck encouraged German families to bear sons who could someday defend the country, Erma recalled her father saying. Bismarck's incentive was 1,000 German marks for every seventh son. So, Otto's birth delivered a windfall of money to the Bergmann family, Erma reported.

Otto Bergmann was a stocky man, built like a wrestler. He was encouraged to climb into the ring but said, "You can't make any money fighting." He went to school to learn to be a butcher and apprenticed in Germany.

Otto served in the German army in Metz, France, from 1906 to 1908, then immigrated to the United States in 1909 at age twenty-three. German emigrants came here in large numbers after the 1848 revolutions in Europe.

He arrived in New York aboard the *Kronprinz Wilhelm*, Erma said. According to Ellis Island records, he was listed as a crewmember on the ship, probably a butcher, Erma thought.

Otto stepped off the boat with the tools of his trade—a sausage maker, a meat saw and a cleaver—swinging from the belt around his waist. He was processed through Ellis Island and then traveled to St. Louis, where three of his brothers owned a bakery on Ohio and LaSalle Streets. Peeling paint spelled "Bergmann's Bakery" on the outside brick wall of their building until it was demolished.

The brothers signed a baking contract with the Civilian Conservation Corps (CCC), a federal jobs program started by President Franklin D. Roosevelt to stimulate the economy. More than three million unemployed, single men served in the CCC during the Depression, from 1933 to 1942. At its peak, about five hundred thousand enrollees worked at more than 2,500 camps run by the federal government.

They planted trees, built roads, fought forest fires and created state and national parks. CCC workers built lodges, trails, fences and museums at Sam Baker, Babler, Washington and Meramec State Parks in Missouri as well as Pere Marquette State Park near Grafton, Illinois. They also took classes to become more employable when the job market picked up.

When Bergmann Bakery landed the contract with the CCC, it moved to Union, Missouri, about fifty miles west of St. Louis. Erma's uncle built a brick home there for his family.

In the meantime, Otto was drafted into the infantry near the end of World War I. He was stationed in Camp Pike, Arkansas, for about eight months. His assignment was to teach his fellow U.S. soldiers how to drill in the German style. He told his family about the animosity toward Germans, as well as his awkward position.

Another of his stories was about his job guarding prisoners, namely the Cuckoo Gang. He later described the gang to his wife and children. The Cuckoo Gang was one of five organized gangs in St. Louis in the early 1900s. They earned a reputation for being fast shooters, with kidnapping and murder their specialties.

Their 1923 mail truck robbery netted the gang $2 million and twenty-five years in prison. Wars among the gangs thinned their ranks. The murder of Cuckoo Gang member Tommy Hayes ended the gang as a force in the St. Louis underground.

About the same time, Sophie Greiner, Erma's mother-to-be, and Sophie's father moved to a flat at 1242 South Broadway in the old French Market area of St. Louis's Soulard neighborhood. Erma's mother was born here in 1893.

During World War I, Erma's mother remembered stuffed toys resembling the kaiser hanging on the lampposts with a sign, "Do you want the kaiser to come over here?" Erma's mother scoffed at the threat, convinced that coming to the United States never entered the kaiser's mind.

Nevertheless, many German Americans rooted for the kaiser. But after Congress declared war against Germany on April 6, 1917, pressure grew to muzzle the slightest German tendencies. Some St. Louis street names were even changed, including Berlin Avenue, which became Pershing; Von Versen Avenue, renamed Enright; Kaiser Avenue, changed to Gresham; and Brunswick Avenue renamed January.

"My grandpa buried three wives," Erma recalled. Erma's mother, Sophie Greiner, was eighteen months old, and her sister Johanna was four years old when his first wife died. Their father then married "Mother Rosa," whose son he adopted. They had two children. Son Frank became a brother in the Catholic Marianist order, and daughter Erma died of diphtheria. He and his third wife had no children.

"Variety is good," Erma remembered her grandfather saying.

Sophie's grandparents opened a tailoring shop on Seventh Street and Chouteau Avenue. She sewed for wealthy women, and he made suits for men. They later moved to Owensville, Missouri, where Sophie captured second prize in a beauty contest while visiting her grandparents, according to family lore.

Sophie studied piano for eight years and specialized in ragtime, the rage at the turn of the twentieth century. Her father bought her a Chilton piano that was shipped from New York. She also had a player piano, and years later, during World War II, she gave both pianos to the army. They were used to entertain servicemen in the USOs.

With music in her makeup, it's no wonder she told Erma about patronizing the St. Louis Bayern Verin (German House) on Lafayette and Jefferson Avenues, where she met her future husband. The couple, dressed in Bavarian costumes, slid across the dance floor to German folk tunes, according to Sophie. They danced the thigh-slapping Schuhplattler. Lederhosen completed Otto's outfit, and Sophie was dressed in her finest: a flowing printed skirt.

Sophie, age thirty, married Otto, thirty-seven, on August 25, 1923, in a simple ceremony at Otto's brother's farm in rural Missouri. The bridegroom moved into the upstairs flat at 1814a South Broadway, where the bride and her father had lived since 1910.

"There were two double beds in the bedroom. Grandpa slept in one and my mother and father slept in the other. Grandpa subsisted on a $9-a-month old age pension," Erma said. He died in 1940.

Sophie was Catholic, and Otto was Lutheran. Sophie assumed that any children born of the marriage would be raised Catholic. Otto had a different idea. He insisted his children attend nearby Trinity Lutheran Church, the oldest Lutheran church west of the Mississippi River. Erma and her brothers went to Sunday school there; their father attended Lutheran services in German.

This division of faiths was a cross Erma's mother carried for the rest of her life, she told Erma. She tearfully visited a priest at Saints Peter and Paul Catholic Church, where she attended 6:00 a.m. Mass every Sunday, regretting her children were not Catholic. Sophie's brother was a Marianist brother, and her aunt was a Notre Dame nun in Germany.

When Erma was in her fifties, she stopped for breakfast at a Schnucks Market at Grand Avenue and Iron Street in South St. Louis. She was on her way home after working the night shift in the St. Louis Police Department. She overheard a conversation among three men. They were talking about Brother Frank. She told them he was her uncle. The three men were Brothers of Mary, too. They said Brother Frank was the most devoted man they knew. "When he died, he went straight to heaven with no stops in between," they told Erma. "Was I proud," Erma boasted, remembering the incident.

Frank celebrated his fiftieth anniversary as a Brother of Mary in 1970 and died shortly after. Erma carried a yellowed card commemorating his jubilee in her heavy purse.

With two religious vocations in her family, Erma leaned toward the Catholic Church. Most of the girls with whom she played baseball were Catholic, and she tagged along with them to Mass on Sundays. But she postponed officially joining the church in case she met a non-Catholic she wanted to marry. She didn't want her children to experience a mixed marriage as she had. And she wanted to be able to share the same religion with her husband. "If we can sleep together, we can go to church together," she reasoned.

In 2000, after her parents died and after the likelihood of marriage and motherhood passed, Erma joined the Catholic Church and faithfully attended Mass at 4:30 on Saturday afternoons at Immaculate Heart of Mary Church.

2

THE BIRTH OF A BALLPLAYER

Ronald Reagan always said he was born in a cold-water flat over a barbershop. I was born in a cold-water flat above a shoe store.
—*Erma Bergmann*

Erma Mary was born on June 18, 1924, a year after Sophie and Otto's wedding and three years after women gained the right to vote in Missouri.

It was a time when Rudolph Valentino and Mary Pickford thrilled moviegoers. George Gershwin wrote *Rhapsody in Blue*, and Calvin Coolidge was the thirtieth president of the United States. America enjoyed ecstatic prosperity. It was the Roaring 'Twenties, and Erma was destined to roar.

The Bergmann family lived at 1814a South Broadway in the Soulard neighborhood. The family occupied the second floor of the building. A living room, dining room, kitchen, bedroom, hall room and bathroom were on the second floor. Buckets of heated water were poured into the claw-foot bathtub.

Erma slept between her mom and dad until she left home to play baseball. Her brother Otto slept on a cot in the dining room, and Victor, the youngest, occupied the hall room. Queenie, the German shepherd, was a gift to Erma's mother from her family doctor. The third floor was an attic with a bedroom in the front. Erma's mother rented the room in the attic for five dollars a month to a butcher, her husband's roommate before his marriage. The renter ate dinner with them most evenings. He lived in the attic until he was eighty-six years old.

Erma's mother also rented the hall room from time to time. Renting rooms to help ends meet was common during the Depression. Young Victor

Erma is five months old in this photo. *Courtesy Erma Bergmann.*

vacated the hall room and joined his brother on another cot in the dining room.

Although most of their neighbors had outhouses, the Bergmanns had indoor plumbing. The pull chain in the box above flushed the toilet and was a constant source of amusement for children in the neighborhood.

The family rented from Balzer Hat Company. The rent was twenty dollars a month in the 1920s; it later increased to thirty dollars a month.

The family celebrated Erma's third birthday in June 1927, the same weekend St. Louisans hailed Charles Lindbergh's triumphant return to town. He spoke to an estimated one hundred thousand people at Forest Park's Art Hill about the city's potential to be an aviation hub. He waved from a white convertible to admirers packed ten deep along the eight-mile parade route from Forest Park to downtown.

Down the street from Erma's house, Mr. Mecklenberg's wooden Indian statue guarded the entrance to his cigar store. As a youngster, Erma bought Mecklenberg's cigars, five for ten cents, for her dad. A treat for him was a King Edward cigar for a nickel. The liquor store was on the next block.

The street was cobblestone and dirt. The city squirted the gutters, and children took advantage of the opportunity to wash their feet. You could shower in the firehouse. The city operated public bathhouses across from Soulard Market. Customers paid two cents for a bar of soap and a towel, Erma remembered.

Duchess Pool Hall was across the street. The Bergmann children looked out their front window and watched the players.

Prohibition marked the beginning of 1920. Flappers with bobbed hair, cloche hats and short skirts danced the Charleston and intoned "How Dry I Am."

Erma's father made wine, and her mother made home-brewed beer in the attic. This was a popular hobby during Prohibition. Erma was sent to the store to buy cans of Banner malt for the beer. Her mother had a bench and a capper for her beer-making enterprise, and the German family enjoyed the fruits of her labors.

It was thirteen long years before Prohibition was repealed. Beer was again legal at 12:01 a.m. on Friday, April 7, 1933. Anheuser-Busch Brewery, near Erma's house, hustled a case of beer to President Franklin D. Roosevelt in the White House in Washington, D.C.

After Prohibition, Erma bought beer for her parents: ten cents for a quart bucket, which was also used for cottage cheese purchased at the nearby dairy. The bartender at Bentrup Restaurant across Broadway from their house filled the aluminum bucket with draft beer. On the way home, Erma flung the container full circle. Even though there was no lid on the bucket, she claims she never spilled a drop of beer.

Erma's drink during these days was Schoenfeld Tea, used as a laxative. She remembers too well the smell wafting from the steaming cup. The pungent odor upset her stomach and made her gag. But it kept her elimination process regular.

Erma remembers going to Das Deutsche Haus, later translated to German House, with her mother, father, grandfather and brother Otto. The St. Louis landmark opened in 1928 on Lafayette and Jefferson Avenues as a German cultural center.

In the 1920s, Erma's father and six other German men opened a packinghouse at Grand and Gravois Avenues with an investment of $50,000. One of the partners, a lawyer, told them to incorporate, then later to dissolve the corporation, reorganize and pay him $100,000. The business sank quickly into bankruptcy, and the lawyer committed suicide, according to the family story.

Otto then worked for a series of small packinghouses during his career as a butcher. He earned nine dollars a week during the Great Depression, Erma said. When he lost his job as a butcher, he delivered circulars in the 1930s. He earned twenty dollars a week in the late 1930s working for Grand Packing Company. He cut heads off sheep. One butcher would throw the sheep down, and the other butcher would cut off its head. They hung pigs by their hind legs then stuck a knife in their jugular veins. Erma remembers her father coming home from work with blood splattered on his clothes and face.

Herbert Hoover had taken office as the thirty-first president of the United States in January 1929, just in time to be held responsible for the stock market crash that same year. Although he assured Americans that the crash was temporary, it soon became evident that the worst was yet to come. Thousands of Americans lost their savings and their homes and were forced into shantytowns that popped up across the country.

Erma is about five years old, and her brother Otto is four. Neither married, and they lived together until Otto's death at age eighty-five. *Courtesy Erma Bergmann.*

Hoover was soundly defeated after one term in office. Franklin Roosevelt enjoyed a landslide victory and succeeded Hoover.

President Roosevelt immediately introduced his New Deal, unprecedented programs for economic recovery. His programs included the Works Progress Administration, which provided employment for skilled and unskilled labor, including artists and musicians. His Public Works Administration erected public buildings and built highways, The Civilian Conservation Corps was aimed at putting young single men to work on conservation projects. The pace was slow, but eventually the New Deal brought the nation out of the Great Depression.

Erma and Otto passed their childhood years in these trying times. Fifteen months after Erma was born, her brother Otto arrived. Erma and Otto played together, went to school together and seemed to be inseparable. Neither of them married, and they lived together their entire lives until Otto's death in 2010 at eighty-five years of age.

When Otto was six years old, he and Erma were walking home from Lafayette Elementary School. A Jewish store owner and neighbor came to his doorway and said to them, "You've got a surprise at home." The youngsters rushed home, climbed the steps to their living quarters and found a little, blond, curly-haired brother lying in a crib under the cuckoo clock, a wedding present from Otto's bachelor roommate, who secured the clock from Germany. Victor joined the family.

"We didn't even know our mother was pregnant," Erma exclaimed.

3

QUEEN OF THE CINDER LOTS

You're born with a talent. But you have to develop it into a skill by repetition.
—Erma Bergmann

Life was simple in the flat. They had two stoves: an oil stove and a wood-and-coal stove. Cooking was done on a combination stove. One side was an oven with gas, and the other side had burners heated by coal. Erma's mother heated the iron on the stove to iron clothes. She scalded the iron bed frames to kill bedbugs.

In 1932, when Erma was eight years old, a coupon in the newspaper entitled a customer to five White Castle hamburgers for ten cents. Admission to the Peerless Picture Show was a dime.

Erma's mother, a pianist, wanted Erma to take piano lessons. But the athletic girl declined, preferring to play outside. "We played with bottle tops and broomsticks. That's how nutty we were about sports. We couldn't afford anything else," Erma recalled, munching a Limburger cheese sandwich. She stood five feet, seven inches tall and weighed about 150 pounds in her prime. Some fifty years later, she still weighed 150 pounds.

Their ball field was a couple of blocks from home at Second Street and Carroll Avenue, across from a lumberyard near the Mississippi River. The field was cobblestone, cinders, dirt and cans. An old bedspring served as a backstop. Flattened cans were bases.

It was a rainy day in August 1939 when a *Star-Times* reporter visited the ball field to watch a girl pitcher who played on a boys' baseball team. This was Erma's first brush with the media.

Rain poured on the cinders and the players. But there were no rain delays for the Phantoms and the Pirates. These two teams, made up of youngsters between the ages of twelve and twenty, battled each other once or twice a week, regardless of the weather.

The story that appeared in the August 14, 1939 edition of the *Star-Times* was headlined "Girl Star Who Shines at a Man's Game." Erma produced the clipping for me. The photograph showed Erma in her windup, with her left leg thrown higher than her head. The girl star had pitched ten straight victories that summer. She was also one of the team's leading hitters.

A youngster on the sidelines identified the player for the reporter. "Erma Bergmann's her name. Pitches all the time for this team. Erma's the best pitcher around these parts," he declared. As the game progressed, the fifteen-year-old's assortment of curves and fastballs confirmed the lad's appraisal. Her fastball sometimes flew past the catcher. The catcher was Pete Randick, her nineteen-year-old boyfriend. The Croatian boy lived in the neighborhood.

"I guess that's about all we do all day in the summer," Erma told the reporter between innings. "Just play ball and catch. We tried to play catch in the alley near our house, but the cop made us stop. So, we got up this team and have been playing our games down here." Ice trucks and horses and wagons with vegetables rolled down the alley, making it dangerous for ballplayers.

Erma remembered two girls from the old neighborhood. One girl brought shiny marbles and a cork-ball bat to the group of kids. "She showed them to us, but she never let us play with them," Erma recalled.

Erma, then a student at McKinley High School, also played softball for the Melber Bakery at St. Louis Softball Park. The reporter asked her if she ever tried out for the boys' team at McKinley. She shook her head and paused a moment. "No," she answered, "But it's an idea."

The Bergmann boys were only mildly athletic. Otto wore glasses and was afraid the ball might hit him in the face and break his glasses. Victor played ball sometimes but never on an organized team. Otto was adept at mathematics, and Victor was mechanically minded. As adults, Otto became a freight salesman, and Victor turned the wheel as a union truck driver.

When Erma wasn't playing ball, she and Otto were busy earning money. "You couldn't ask for money, so we went junking and sold tin cans," Erma said. "We cruised the ash pits to find things we could sell. We spent the money on things like a pack of gum or a Coke that cost a penny or a nickel."

This was the decade of the Great Depression. Nearby two-room apartments with outhouses on Russell Avenue rented for $6 a month, or 20¢ a day. A new car cost about $525 in 1937.

There was a floral shop across the street from the Bergmann flat. Erma worked there, earning $2.50 a week washing floors, cleaning vases, scrubbing steps and delivering flowers on the bus after school and on Saturdays. The son of the owner secured an appointment to a military academy and was the envy of the neighborhood, Erma recalled.

On Saturdays, Erma ran errands and earned twenty-five cents for scrubbing a wooden, two-seater outdoor toilet behind their landlord's hat store. "There were twenty-four steps to our flat upstairs. I know because I scrubbed them every Saturday," said the future pitcher.

Several trucking companies were located near the Bergmann flat, and Erma and her brothers visited them frequently. Otto was fifteen years old when one of the regular drivers was assigned the job of picking up a load of canned milk in Litchfield, Illinois, fifty-two miles from St. Louis. The driver decided he didn't want to make the trip, so he asked Otto to do it for him. Erma and Otto did most things together, so Erma was enlisted to go along.

An elderly gentleman in their neighborhood taught Erma how to drive a stick shift on his old car. Otto let Erma drive the tractor that pulled a trailer down the highway. Erma turned off the highway onto a road that led to their destination. Out of the corner of her eye, she saw a policeman in his car watching her turn. Panic gripped her heart like icy fingers around her neck. She didn't have a driver's license. How would she explain their mission to the policeman?

"If we had been thrown in jail, my mother would have been so upset," she said, horrified at the thought.

The policeman ignored them, and Erma proceeded down the road to the loading dock. Otto took the wheel and attempted unsuccessfully to back the trailer close to the dock. Erma remembered hearing the truck drivers say that you needed to turn the wheel the opposite direction of the way you wanted the trailer to go. Looking back over her right shoulder, she whipped the wheel to the right, and the trailer nudged its way up to the dock. The pair loaded the milk and returned to St. Louis.

In another motorized incident, Erma and Otto were riding in the Bergmann pickup truck with Benny Fritz, a friend of their parents. Benny was a driver for Peterson Feed Company, located in their neighborhood. When they had a flat tire, the two men told Erma to crawl under the truck and place the jack under the truck's frame. Neither of the men seemed to know how to do it. So Erma crawled on her stomach under the truck while the other two watched. After the tire was changed, Otto and Benny climbed into the cab. Erma returned to her seat in the open bed of the truck. The threesome continued on their journey.

While passing through Waterloo, Illinois, about ten miles from St. Louis, the truck hit a hole in the street. Erma bounced out of the open truck and onto the street. Her nose was broken, and her forehead was cut. Blood flowed from both injuries. She lost consciousness for a moment. When she regained her senses, she saw Benny wringing his hands and muttering about his being arrested on the Mann Act. The accident happened in front of the county courthouse.

The Mann Act, officially known as the White Slave Traffic Act of 1910, forbids transporting a minor across state lines for the purpose of prostitution. Congressman James R. Mann had introduced the law, and it became better known by his name. Erma was sixteen years old, and they had indeed crossed the state line from Missouri into neighboring Illinois. Erma commanded Benny, "Quit worrying about the Mann Act and get me a drink of water." Erma's injuries from the accident healed, and she resumed her busy life.

Erma remembers an old man with a bucket, mop and squeegee washing store windows for twenty-five cents. "Then he bought a bottle of wine," she added. "Living in the old neighborhood helped me with my police work. I knew how the poor people lived. I saw guys eat out of garbage cans during the Depression," she added.

Originally, Germans owned the Broadway businesses. After World War I, Jewish shopkeepers moved in. It was a busy neighborhood. The Bergmanns brought chairs out and sat on the front sidewalk to watch the activity. Streetcars rumbled down Broadway. The bank across the street had U.S. savings bond drives during World War II, with entertainment on a stage set up in front of the bank. The Bergmanns had box seats on the sidewalk.

The kids knew how to split wood and were paid ten cents for a bushel of kindling wood. Erma and Otto hauled two hundred bushels of kindling wood and bought a fancy twenty-dollar bicycle at Sears, Roebuck and Company. The sister and brother shared the bike with each other and with their friends.

In later years, the brother and sister knew how to work for their money and enjoy the fruits of their labors. Otto bought a 1952 Chevrolet for $2,700 in cash, followed by six new Cadillacs through the years. He never married and traveled all over the world, sometimes flying in the four-engine propeller plane he and a group of investors purchased. The plane carried up to ninety-eight passengers and was flown by a retired four-stripe navy pilot. Groups chartered the plane, which flew nonstop to Las Vegas, Alaska, resorts in Mexico and Prince Edward Island in Canada. On one trip, a band played aboard the plane, according to Otto.

Erma graduated six months ahead of time from Lafayette Grade School because she could do long division. She proudly remembers having the third-highest IQ in grade school, although she rarely opened a book. She graduated in January instead of June at thirteen and a half years of age.

"You could have eaten off the floor at Lafayette School," Erma said in later years. "It's a shame the way they let it run down."

Erma taught Otto long division, and he, too, was promoted to the next grade and graduated six months ahead of time. If anyone picked a fight with Otto, he hid behind his big sister. She wasn't a fighter, but she seemed to be able to ward off any violence and protect her brother.

Erma entered McKinley High School. The school was a beautiful piece of architecture designed by William Ittner, who designed hundreds of school buildings throughout the country, many in St. Louis. His schools are still architectural gems one hundred years later.

She wasn't accepted socially at McKinley, because the other girls had better clothes and more spending money. There were cliques, and not everyone belonged. Erma was quiet and retiring in high school. "It never bothered me too much. I always had confidence and never felt inferior. They may have had more material things, but that didn't make them any better," Erma commented.

After the other students discovered her athletic abilities, her acceptance escalated. "I had a lot of confidence playing ball. I never backed away in sports," Erma said. "I didn't like school, but I decided to stick it out. I got math and science, but I failed English literature."

She played trombone in the high school band, and music became her second love after sports. She whirled around doing the jitterbug.

Every year in the early 1940s, St. Louis had a Clean-Up Parade downtown. School bands marched in the parade. Erma and the other trombonists were in the first row of McKinley's marching band, behind the drum majorettes. The players slid their instruments into the air,

Erma graduated from McKinley High School in St. Louis in 1942. *Courtesy Erma Bergmann.*

McKinley dedicated a locker to Erma when the school celebrated its centennial in 2004. Erma attended the festivities. *Courtesy Erma Bergmann.*

and their gold trombones gleamed in the sun. Paul Whiteman was the parade marshal, bedecked in a mustard-colored suit. "That was pretty unusual, because musicians wore dark suits then," Erma commented with a vivid memory of the parade.

Erma graduated from McKinley in January 1942. She is the only person in her family to graduate high school. Otto quit after a year and a half. At age forty, he passed his General Equivalency Diploma (GED) test, the equivalent of a high school diploma.

McKinley high school dedicated a locker to Erma when the school celebrated its one hundredth anniversary in 2004. Erma went back to her high school to accept the honor and to celebrate the school's centennial. McKinley High School also celebrated her success.

4

GROWING UP

Money was never my god, but I wanted to rise above where I grew up.
—Erma Bergmann

Erma had few regrets in life, but one is not being able to go to college. Her dream was to attend the University of Missouri in Columbia and earn a degree in physical education. She knew some students there. They told her that some of the girls working for a physical education degree had little ability in athletics. Erma had the brains and the athletic acumen for college, but her family didn't have the money to send her. Even late in life, despite her successes, other people's educational attainments impressed her, and she bemoaned her lack of schooling.

"I'll join the U.S. Marines. I'm adventuresome in the heart," Erma said to herself. Her long-range plan was to attend college on the GI Bill after her discharge. After World War II, men and women in the armed services could go to school, and the tuition was paid by the government.

In the meantime, her brother Otto, then eighteen years old, was drafted and instructed to report to Jefferson Barracks. He chose the U.S. Marine Corps and was sent to their recruiting office downtown. In those days, if you lived west of the Mississippi River, you went to San Diego for boot camp. If you were east of the river, you were sent to Parris Island, South Carolina.

After his orientation, Otto joined a platoon for additional training to be one of the marines who guarded ships. This required him to swim 150 feet. He and Erma had never learned to swim.

Near their house, Pontiac Square's public swimming pool beckoned youngsters to cool off during the sizzling St. Louis summers. But Otto's

Erma looks quite
distinguished at age twenty.
Courtesy Erma Bergmann.

mother feared that her children would catch a disease from the germs in the water. Erma begged her mother to let her swim there, and Sophie finally relented. Erma contracted head lice, and that squelched her swimming. The pool was forever off-limits for the Bergmann children.

Otto took a physical for infantry training but couldn't pass the eye test. After eight months in service, he was honorably discharged and given $100. "I hitchhiked home," Otto said. When Erma saw how distraught her mother was about the possibility of Otto being killed or hurt in service, she decided against enlisting. Instead, she enrolled at Midland Institute of Commerce, a business school then at Seventh and Pine Streets in downtown St. Louis. She studied typing, shorthand and bookkeeping. A classmate was Betty Streckfus, daughter of John S. Streckfus of Streckfus Steamers Inc., the owner of a fleet of excursion boats that plied the Mississippi River.

His fleet included the popular *Admiral*, which cruised the Mississippi at St. Louis from 1940 to 1978. That's when the U.S. Coast Guard discovered holes in its hull. The sparkling steel steamer that carried four thousand passengers glided on its last nautical mile. In the early 1940s, there wasn't another vessel that equaled the *Admiral* in seamanship and luxury. Erma relished the fact that she knew a member of the owner's family.

Erma landed a stenographer's job at Missouri, Colorado and Kansas Truck Lines (MC&K) and earned forty cents an hour, or sixteen dollars a week. At the same time, her softball career flourished. She was fourteen years old when she joined an amateur softball league. The man who ran a junkyard in the neighborhood asked her to play on his team. This was the beginning of her eight-year career in organized softball at the St. Louis Softball Park.

In the early 1940s, the National Amateur Athletic Union (NAAU) held its annual competition in Atlantic City, New Jersey. One of the events was a long-distance softball throw. An NAAU official thought Erma might be able to beat the record. She stood on the foul line at Shenandoah Park and threw the softball across the grass from right field to left field. They measured her mighty throw, and it was impressive. Unfortunately, the event was canceled because of World War II, and her entry was never recorded. "That was too bad," she bemoaned. "I could have been recognized as an individual, and not just as a team member."

She played amateur softball for George Weick Funeral Home on South Grand near the Pelican Restaurant, a south side landmark in St. Louis. The Weick-sponsored team traveled by rail from St. Louis to games in Peoria and Litchfield via the Illinois Traction System, later called the Illinois Terminal System.

The electric interurban train carried passengers from St. Louis to Illinois towns from 1901 to 1958. In the 1930s, the commuter railroad's downtown station dipped below street level. Six blocks of Twelfth Street, now Tucker Boulevard, were supported by steel stilts while the commuter cars rumbled below. The downtown station was excavated in 2010 as part of a project to connect downtown to a new bridge being built over the Mississippi River.

In Erma's early traveling days, she remembered the Illinois Terminal Railroad operating parlor-car and sleeping-car services with style and panache. Parlor cars sported mahogany wood trim and large, comfortable leather-upholstered chairs, luxuries that amazed Erma.

Mr. Weick gave each ballplayer five dollars in meal money, a generous allowance in 1944. They returned home the same day after the game. Years later, when Erma made funeral arrangements for her father, she met Tom Kutis Jr. of Kutis Funeral Home. He said he wished she had played for his establishment. Erma said, "I would have been glad to play for you, Tommie, but Mr. Weick asked me." The Weick Funeral Home Team was City and Park Champions in 1943, and the team photo appeared in the *Bugle*, a South St. Louis neighborhood newspaper.

Erma played third base and outfield, her strong arm drilling the ball into her teammates' gloves. She was not a fast runner. In fact, a fan stopped her after a game one day and said, "You run like a sewing machine."

"What do you mean?" Erma asked.

"You run in one place too long, but you've got good hands," he explained to the third baseman.

She was about fifteen or sixteen years old when she was asked to play an exhibition game in Chicago. The other girls on the team were between twenty and twenty-two. Her mother said no, but her father said, "Why don't you let her go? She always tells the truth." He persuaded her mother to change her mind.

Erma overheard her father's remark and was so touched that she made sure she behaved in Chicago. The girls rode the train to the Windy City. After the game, the team spent the night in a hotel. Erma went directly to her room and didn't even venture out in the hall for fear of getting in trouble. The team returned to St. Louis via the rails the next day. The experience was a memorable one for the teenager.

Tom Shelley, a welder for General Motors, was one of her softball managers. Occasionally, he and his wife, Fairy, invited some of the girls to their home in the Carondelet area of St. Louis. World War II raged in Europe and Asia, and the Shelleys invited some servicemen who were passing through Jefferson Barracks on the way to their assignments. Erma was beginning to develop social contacts outside of the old neighborhood.

Erma and many St. Louisans packed the Casa Loma Ballroom, which had opened in South St. Louis in 1935. Artie Shaw, Ray Anthony, Tommy Dorsey, Glenn Miller and Guy Lombardo and his Royal Canadians were some of the big bands that struck a steady beat as couples strutted across the dance floor.

One evening, Erma and three girlfriends paid the admission charge and climbed the flight of steps to the ballroom. A well-to-do gentleman asked Erma to dance. He asked her again and again, and the two of them danced with each other for two sets of music. He asked her where she lived, and she told him on South Broadway between Russell and Lafayette. He was appalled that she lived in such a poor neighborhood. He made a quick sidestep exit from the dance floor after telling her he was high-class and lived in Walnut Park. His neighborhood was an upper-middle-class section of St. Louis. He disappeared after digesting the fact that she was from South Broadway. She later laughed about his informing her that he was high-class. "I was told I had pretty legs and a good figure. It never bought me anything, but it was nice to hear," Erma smiled.

Erma's escorts took her to the 400 Club, a dance hall near Grand and Delmar, and the Club Plantation dance hall on Enright Avenue across from the current John Cochran VA Hospital. The Club Plantation, popular in the 1940s, was in the Palladium building, which opened in 1914 as a roller rink. Dancers jitterbugged across the wood parquet floor where roller skaters had glided when the building opened.

On special dates, Erma got dressed up and went to the Chase Club, the premier entertainment spot in St. Louis from the 1940s to the 1970s. It was the pulsing heart of the Chase Park Plaza Hotel. The late Jack Buck, longtime St. Louis Baseball Cardinals announcer, said, "The Chase was the Mecca for everything in St. Louis—where the elite used to meet and cheat." There was Erma in the midst of the excitement at the Chase.

World War II challenged the American people and brought them together. The government found it necessary to ration food, sugar, gasoline, tires, fuel oil and even clothing. Nylon stockings were coveted commodities. Folks over the age of sixteen could apply for books of ration stamps every six months. If a consumer ran out of stamps for the month, he or she had to wait until the next month to buy more of the rationed goods. Sometimes, people traded with neighbors if they used less gasoline or food.

Americans conserved everything for the war effort. Few people complained, because they knew it was the men and women in uniform who were making the greater sacrifice. A government poster read, "Do with less so they'll have enough."

Rationing ended in 1945, the year Erma and her two brothers boarded a Greyhound bus and traveled two thousand miles to Hollywood, California, via Route 66 to visit their aunt and uncle, who owned a drive-in meat market. They got as far as Kansas City and had to give up their seats on the bus, since servicemen had priority. The three travelers would get up to the bus door ready to step inside, when several army personnel would brush them aside and take their seats. They spent the night on benches in the bus depot. "We dusted every bench in the station," Erma laughed. But when they finally arrived in Hollywood, the threesome was thrilled to see movie stars drive up to their aunt and uncle's meat market.

A severe case of homesickness afflicted this fearless female on her first trip away from home. "I wanted to jump over the Rocky Mountains to get back home," Erma said, remembering vividly the painful experience.

At the outset of World War II, trouble had begun to brew in the world of Major League Baseball. Young men eighteen years of age and older were serving in the armed services. Four million fighters served during World War II. Many Minor League Baseball teams had to disband because of a lack of personnel. Baseball minds wondered about the future of major league parks.

The Honorable Kenesaw Landis, a Chicago judge and the commissioner of baseball, wrote to President Franklin Roosevelt about the uncertain future of America's pastime. In his reply of January 15, 1942, the president heartily cheered the continuation of baseball.

Here are excerpts of his letter, published by the MLB in its history.

I honestly feel that it would be best for the country to keep baseball going. There will be fewer people unemployed and everybody will work longer hours and harder than ever before. And that means that they ought to have a chance for recreation and for taking their minds off their work even more than before.

Baseball provides a recreation which does not last over two hours or two hours and a half, and which can be got for very little cost. And, incidentally, I hope that night games can be extended because it gives an opportunity to the day shift to see a game occasionally.

Very sincerely yours,
[signed] *Franklin D. Roosevelt*
President of the United States

Philip K. Wrigley, the chewing-gum tycoon, stepped up to the plate. He had begun his career in his father's gum company in 1915. Ten years later, he became president of the William Wrigley Jr. Chewing Gum Company. When his father died in 1932, Philip inherited the Chicago Cubs franchise and about four hundred thousand shares of Wrigley stock, valued at about four dollars a share. During his youth, he was a sportsman who enjoyed horseback riding and sailing.

When the Japanese bombed the battleship *Arizona* in Pearl Harbor in December 1941, the United States officially entered World War II. By 1943, it was predicted that three to four million men would go into uniform and millions more would transfer from their nonessential occupations to war-related jobs. This societal change forced by World War II did not bode well for the future of Major League Baseball.

Philip Wrigley organized a committee to come up with a way to keep baseball in business. In the meantime, the gum enterprise was lucrative, and Wrigley was able to allocate $100,000 toward the creation of a professional women's softball league. The All-American Girls Softball League may not have been exactly what President Roosevelt had in mind when he wrote his letter, but it was a way to keep Wrigley Field in operation and ball games going despite fewer male players. And the organizers felt they had the blessing of the White House.

Philip Wrigley's intent was to contribute something to the public and to raise the players' social standing. The women were not only highly skilled players but also excellent examples of good, clean American girlhood. The players were highly respected in their communities. When the players signed their contracts, they agreed to comply with high moral standards and rules of conduct imposed by the league.

Wrigley presented his committee's plan to the National League's team owners and asked if they would let the women play in their stadiums when the men's teams were on the road. The owners said no. They were afraid that baseball fans didn't have the time or money to support both men's and women's games. So Wrigley turned from large metropolitan areas to medium-sized cities closer to his home base. His network of baseball recruiters invited 280 softball players to the final tryouts in Chicago, where 60 were chosen to become the first women to play professional baseball.

Tryouts were held at Wrigley Field in Chicago. Female athletes sprinted out on the diamond in the spring of 1943. Philip Wrigley's media campaign reinforced the players' femininity and emphasized their patriotic purpose of providing recreation for war workers. His media plan was effective, and the league was featured in national publications such as *Time*, *Life*, *Collier's* and *McCall's* and received regular coverage in league cities' newspapers.

Four teams of sixty-four players in the new women's league competed in 108 games and drew 176,000 fans. In the next few years, under the tutoring of managers who had played Major League Baseball, the game evolved from softball to baseball.

While some female sports figures seem to be tough on the outside, these ladies were feminine on the exterior. And some, like Erma, were tough on the inside. During their playing days, they were required to act like ladies and play ball like men. Femininity and attractiveness were key components of Wrigley's recruiting criteria.

His uniform committee, which included his wife, Helen, was charged with creating a new outfit that was more feminine than the softball uniforms the players were accustomed to wearing. Their final design was inspired by field hockey and figure skating outfits of the 1940s. The players would wear a one-piece dress with a three-quarter-length flared skirt that covered satin briefs. The skirt resembled a ballerina's covering, but the players' stage was a diamond. Their socks reached just under their knees, but their thighs were uncovered. Base stealers bemoaned the bumps and bruises on bare legs. Their legs sometimes looked like a fresh strawberry with rough and bleeding thighs. These injuries were thus nicknamed "strawberries." Chaperones applied peroxide and bandaging to many strawberries.

When a player signed a contract with the league, she agreed to keep herself in first-class physical condition and conform to high standards of good citizenship, good sportsmanship and personal conduct.

When the league started, Philip Wrigley was selling a wholesome product to midwestern fans, and the players' ladylike image was part of the package. Players were not allowed to smoke, drink or wear pants in public. Short hair was also taboo. All social engagements, living quarters and eating places had to be approved by the chaperones. Any infringement of the rules of conduct resulted in a fine: five dollars for a first offense, ten dollars for the second and suspension for the third infraction. Wrigley felt that if his baseball players maintained their feminine dignity, it would increase their appeal and the league's chance for success.

His example may have been Mildred Burke, women's wrestling champion from 1937 to 1954. She was the longest-reigning female wrestling champion. Her resolve was to be a lady first and a champion wrestler second, according to her biography. Her muscles rippled and her diamonds sparkled. She conducted a world tour and enjoyed a hero's welcome.

Wrigley hired instructors from the Helena Rubinstein Salon in 1943 and the Ruth Tiffany School in 1944 to teach evening charm school. At spring training, when days were filled with batting practice and fielding and pitching drills, the women went to night school to work on their charm. The players were coached in the arts of walking, sitting, speaking, selecting clothes and applying makeup.

Their responsibility was to project a feminine image when appearing in public. Apparently, the ladies did a good job. Some players felt like sailors with a suitor in every port. Gentlemen were waiting at the ballparks when the teams arrived to play ball.

Phil Wrigley's media campaign pitched themes like "Recreation for War Workers," "Femininity," "Community Welfare" and "Family Entertainment." This publicity helped the public accept these female players. It must have worked, because Erma never detected any criticism.

Finding a league name that pleased everyone was another challenge. The ladies played under MLB rules, so the league was renamed the All-American Girls Baseball League. But they used shorter baselines, underhand pitching and (soft) oversized balls. So, in 1945, it became the All-American Girls Professional Ball League. This was the same year Doris Day sang her first hit, "Sentimental Journey," recorded with the Les Brown Band.

In the late 1940s, pitching switched to overhand, the ball gradually shrank to baseball size and the baselines grew. The distance between home plate and the pitcher' s mound was stretched to sixty feet, six inches, the same length that Bob Gibson, the St. Louis Cardinals Hall of Fame pitcher, hurled the ball.

When the players were recognized by the National Baseball Hall of Fame in Cooperstown, New York, in 1988, they were known as the All-American Girls Professional Baseball League, a name that accurately describes their game.

In 1875, the first female baseball players to play for money marched onto the field in Springfield, Illinois. Two teams, the Blondes and the

Brunettes, traveled to South Indiana, Chicago and New York to play ball and entertain sports fans.

Through the years, a handful of women made their marks as players, including Alta Weiss, the "girl wonder." At age sixteen in 1907, she made her professional debut, pitching a sinking fastball in a men's semipro league. She gave up only four hits and one run in five innings. She pitched her way through Starling Ohio Medical College, the only woman in the class of 1914. Alta routinely drew more than three thousand people to watch her pitch, and she played ball well into the Roaring Twenties. At the same time, she treated patients as a practicing physician.

Lizzie Murphy played for nearly thirty years with the Bloomer Girls. She made baseball history in 1922 in a two-inning appearance for the American League All-Stars against the Boston Red Sox. She was the first woman to play Major League Baseball.

So, the All-American Girls Professional Baseball League of the 1940s and 1950s had some formidable spikes to fill. Fans in the Midwest welcomed the teams, and the games helped steer their minds away from the war.

Thirty scouts from the new league hired by Phil Wrigley recruited the best softball players in the United States and Canada. It was a hot summer night at the St. Louis Softball Park in 1945 when scout Albert Nicolai sat in the stands watching the game. Erma played third base, knees slightly bent, eyes on the batter. She scooped up a ground ball and fired it across the diamond to Mayme Raines, who played first base.

"I always hoped every ball would be hit to Erma," eighty-seven-yearold Mayme recalled. "She wouldn't lob it to me, she really threw it. She was a good hitter, too. She was an all-around good ball player," said Mayme, a pleasant, gray-haired lady peering through oversized glasses.

Mayme became a bride in 1936. She was one of only two married ballplayers. Her husband was away in the service, and Mayme lived with her father-in-law. He didn't know she smoked until Erma came bouncing into their house one day and yelled, "Have you got a fag?" The two women collapsed in laughter, remembering the incident while they talked about the old days over lunch at the Elephant Bar in West St. Louis County. It had been more than sixty years since they played ball together, and they didn't recognize each other when they first met up again. But their shared memories melted the years.

Mayme had two children, a girl and a boy. Her daughter Pat had lunch with us. Pat grew up at the ballpark. "I watched my mother play ball from the time I could walk until I was about ten years old," Pat said. How surprised and slightly disappointed Mayme must have been when, years later, she watched her daughter play mediocre softball on the Brown Shoe Company team.

Mayme played until she was thirty years old and six months pregnant with Pat's brother, Billy, who was born almost twelve years after Pat.

"Erma and I were pretty good buddies. We went out together and quite often she came over to our house on Sidney Street near Broadway," Mayme said. The girls patronized Koenig's, a tavern on Virginia Avenue in South St. Louis. Koenig's had a jukebox and a dance floor. A three-piece band beat out the tempo for the dancers on some weekend nights. Erma and Mayme twirled around the floor, dancing the jitterbug. "We used to have a lot of fun," Mayme said, enjoying the memories.

The former softball players recalled a game when Erma was running from third base to the plate. The catcher blocked the plate and knocked Erma down. When she tried to get up, she was knocked down again. Erma squared off to retaliate when the catcher's father came off the bench and said, "I'm glad you called her bluff."

When scout Nicolai talked to Erma about joining the new women's league, she knew very little about it. But she had heard that Audrey Kissel, another St. Louisan, was playing in the league. She didn't know Audrey then, but they met about fifty years later at a league reunion. The two former ballplayers became bosom buddies. Since Erma did not have cable television service, she often went to Audrey's house to watch St. Louis Cardinals games.

Audrey grew up tagging along with three older brothers who played softball and baseball. "They really coached me well," she said years later when she was interviewed by the league. When Audrey was recruited for the big league, her mother opposed the idea. Audrey knew another girl who had played the previous season. The two mothers talked, and Audrey's mother was assured her daughter would be safe, that the girls were chaperoned and were closely watched. So her mother agreed to let her go.

She joined the league in 1944 and played second base for the Minneapolis Millerettes. The team took the field for their first home game against the Rockford Peaches at Nicollet Park on May 27, 1944. The United Press covered the game and patronized the players instead of reporting on their skills. "Quick, Millie, my mask and mascara, for there's a powder puff plot underway which threatens the foundation of the national pastime, a conspiracy aimed at virtual extinction of the perspiring, swearing, tobacco-chewing baseball player," reported the United Press.

After the home opener, sports reporter Halsey Hall was a bit more respectful of the women as players, describing the action as it was occurring. "In a welter of flaring skirts, headlong and feet-first slides into base, bodily contact, good pitching, and really brilliant outfielding."

Audrey played with some outstanding ballplayers that year. Dorothy Wiltse Collins was one of the best pitchers in the history of the league. In 1945, she pitched two games of a doubleheader for the Fort Wayne Daisies and won them both.

Faye Dancer was an exceptional athlete and an entertainer on the field. Out in center field, she would perform cartwheels, splits and handstands. Off the field, she played tricks on other players and especially on new chaperones. Her teammates remembered her replacing the cream in the chaperone's Oreos with toothpaste. It's not surprising that Faye Dancer was the inspiration for Madonna's "All the Way Mae" character in *A League of Their Own*.

During a game in South Bend, Indiana, Audrey was spiked on the side of her knee by a runner attempting to slip into second base without being tagged out. Audrey thought the injury was deliberate, and she ran after the offender. Her teammates held the five-foot, two-inch second baseman in tow until she composed herself. The cut on the side of her knee required seven stitches. Her chaperone accompanied her to the hospital, and the chaperone fainted when they gave Audrey the shots to numb the knee. Audrey was out of the game for about two weeks. "They practically had to tie me to the bench. I wanted to get out there and play." She was spiked again in the same season, this time by her own teammate. Her center fielder came crashing in chasing a fly ball and collided with Audrey, her spike catching her leg. "I wondered where she came from," Audrey recalled.

Audrey's rathskeller, or finished basement, in her compact three-bedroom home in St. Louis County is a treasure trove of memorabilia from her baseball career. Her glove, baseballs, pictures, baseball contract, newspaper articles and awards are some of the historic artifacts in her museum. She even has the pink ribbons she wore in her hair, inspiring the press to call her "Pigtails." Her baseball salary was sixty dollars a week, a whopping increase over the ten dollars a week she earned working at a bakery. Some of the players earned more than their fathers.

"Our uniforms were pink with burgundy hats, burgundy shorts (bloomers), burgundy socks and a burgundy belt," Audrey told the *St. Louis Post-Dispatch* in a July 2, 1992 article, "Ladies in Gloves." When a player ended her career, she surrendered her uniform to her team. The article appeared a few weeks after the movie *A League of Their Own* opened in theaters across the country.

Erma told the writer, "I never dreamt it would be what it actually was. It was one of the greatest experiences, I think, that a young girl could have at that time in sports."

Audrey laughs when she remembers watching her teammates learn to walk balancing books on their heads during the two-week evening charm school. Phil Wrigley hired the Ruth Tiffany Charm School of Chicago to coach his girls. The Helena Rubinstein Cosmetics Company taught the athletes how to put on makeup, get in and out of a car and put on a coat with grace. To avoid getting dirt under their fingernails when sliding on the base paths, they were told to scratch a bar of soap before the game.

"It helped me a lot," Audrey said. "I played ball since I was five years old. I was always a tomboy," she said. The players agreed. "They wanted us to play like men but look and act like women."

As a matter of fact, the league published "Rules of Conduct for Players." The management expected the ladies to live up to the code of conduct they specified in writing:

> ALWAYS appear in feminine attire when not actively engaged in practice or playing ball. At no time may a player appear in the stands in her uniform, or wear slacks or shorts in public.
>
> Boyish bobs are not permissible. Your hair should be well groomed at all times, with longer hair preferable to short haircuts. Lipstick should always be on.
>
> Smoking or drinking are not permitted in public places. Obscene language will not be tolerated.
>
> All social engagements must be approved by the chaperones.
>
> Jewelry must not be worn during games or practices.
>
> All living quarters and eating places must be approved by the chaperone.
>
> For emergency purposes, it is necessary that you leave notice of your whereabouts and your home phone.
>
> Each club will establish a satisfactory place to eat, and a time when all members must be in their individual rooms.
>
> In general, the lapse of time will be two hours after the finish of the last game, but in no case, later than 12:30 a.m.

The rules also specified that uniform skirts should not be shorter than six inches above the kneecap. Fines of five dollars for a first offense, ten dollars for a second offense and suspension for a third offense were automatically imposed for breaking any of the rules.

During the season, Audrey was notified by the U.S. Navy that her fiancé pilot had been shot down over Japanese-held territory and was missing in action. She was devastated by the news and toyed with the idea of continuing her baseball career. She loved the game and was deliberating about signing a contract for the 1945 season when she received a telegram from Bremerton, Washington. Fred Lafser had been rescued. She left her job at McQuay Norris working on a secret defense project, placed her unsigned baseball contract aside and headed downtown to buy a wedding dress.

She married Freddie on his thirty-day leave. The couple had five children. They attended league reunions together, and Fred enjoyed them as much as Audrey did. After fifty-five years of marriage, Fred died suddenly in 2000. Audrey had nine grandchildren and seven great-grandchildren. One of her passions was watching St. Louis Cardinals games on television.

In 1943, the All-American Girls All-Star Game at Wrigley Field in Chicago doubled as a recruiting drive for the Women's Army Corps, or WACs. The summer Audrey joined the league, the four teams played under special portable lights set up for the nighttime doubleheader. These were the first games ever played after dark at Wrigley Field. There was free admission for Red Cross workers, people who donated blood through the Red Cross and armed forces personnel. In 1988, more than four decades later, permanent lights were erected, and night games for the Cubs began in Chicago.

After the 1944 season, as the war effort was winding down, Philip Wrigley predicted the return of the popularity of men's Major League Baseball and was convinced the government would not shut it down. He sold the women's league to his advertising director, Arthur Meyerhoff, who guided the league's affairs during its most successful period. Ownership of the individual teams went to franchises.

Back in St. Louis in 1945, the manager of the St. Louis Softball Park discouraged Erma from accepting Nicolai's offer. He told her she would lose her amateur status and would be barred from playing in the softball league for two years if she didn't make it in baseball.

Erma was a draw, and he needed her to bring in the fans, who paid ten cents admission. He implied that Nicolai's promise of fame and fortune was a hoax. Erma was disappointed. She expected to be lauded with cheers and congratulations. She could hardly believe how discouraging the softball park manager was about her becoming a professional baseball player.

Erma was torn, like the dried wishbone on the Thanksgiving turkey. She loved the softball league—the lights, the field, the popcorn, the umpires, the crowd. The possibility of not being able to play softball if she didn't make the big league sent a shudder up her spine.

She turned Nicolai down and stayed on the softball field. That same year, Germany surrendered, and May 8 was declared Victory in Europe (V-E) Day. Japan surrendered, and September 2, 1945, became Victory in Japan (V-J) Day.

President Roosevelt died at his home in Warm Springs, Georgia, and Vice President Harry S. Truman became president. Penicillin was discovered, *Going My Way* won the Oscar for Best Picture and Bess Myerson was crowned 1945's Miss America.

The next year, scout Albert Nicolai talked to Erma again. She was still hesitant and asked him, "Where will I sleep and what will I eat?" He told her she would earn $75.00 a week plus $3.50 per day meal money when she played on the road. This was quite a windfall compared to her $16.00 a week stenographer's salary at the trucking company. The prospect of making that much money playing a game she loved was as irresistible as a root beer float on a hot St. Louis summer day.

Erma decided to try it. She told her mother, "If it's fake, I'll be back on the first bus or train." Her mother, always her biggest cheerleader, sent Erma to baseball camp with her full support.

Albert Nicolai tucked $100 in his pocket for recruiting Erma. When the league scout died in St. Louis in 1984 at the age of eighty-seven, Erma went to his funeral. She never forgot the man who changed the course of her life.

5

BATTER UP, BERGIE

Hit that ball so far they'll never find it.
—Sophie Bergmann, Erma's mother

It was 1946. It cost a nickel to mail a letter. Chrysler Corporation debuted the 1946 Town and Country convertible with then-in-vogue wood-panel flanks that looked as good on a drop-top as they did on a station wagon. This eye-popping model cost $2,998 and was second only to the Crown Imperial as Chrysler's most expensive model.

Thankfully, World War II had finally ended. So had the baseball girls' charm school. Erma was grateful for that, too.

Twenty-one-year-old Erma stepped off the train in Pascagoula, Mississippi, ready to report to training camp. The sun caught the auburn highlights in her brown hair. Her green eyes sparkled with excitement. She was one of about one hundred new prospects signed by the league during the winter. These rookies joined the old-timers from the last three years at this picturesque resort on the Gulf of Mexico near Biloxi. The rookies and pitchers reported on April 25; the veterans arrived a week later. "I felt like an east-side kid who went west," Erma remembered.

She hoisted her suitcase, which held her Marty Marion glove, her spike shoes and other earthly possessions. Erma played with this glove her entire career, and it's now among her baseball mementos. "I told my nephew he should have this glove bronzed," she said. Marty Marion played shortstop for the St. Louis Cardinals from 1940 to 1950. He played on four National

League pennant-winning teams and three World Series Championship teams in the 1940s. The women's league furnished uniforms, but players supplied their own gloves and spikes.

Erma was confident about making the league and anxious to show her stuff. After all, the previous year, hadn't she been chosen to play third base for the All-Star Team, composed of the best ballplayers from all the girls' softball teams in St. Louis? And hadn't Mr. Nicolai, the recruiter, pursued her two years in a row?

Soon after she stepped onto the baseball diamond in Pascagoula, Erma knew she made the grade. She also learned she liked grits, coarsely ground hominy that is a staple of breakfasts throughout the South.

"Erma Bergmann is one of the top rookies this year," said Max Carey, president of the All-American Girls Professional Baseball League (AAGPBL) from 1945 to 1949. Carey played in the major leagues for twenty years for the Pittsburgh Pirates and the Brooklyn Dodgers and was one of the greatest outfielders of his time. He held the NL record for stolen bases and later was inducted into the National Baseball Hall of Fame.

Phil Wrigley hired former major league players to manage the women's teams. Max Carey was the only manager who went on to serve as president of the league as well. After the league dissolved, Carey moved to Miami Beach, Florida, to manage a dog track. Erma visited him at his Florida home and attended the dog races.

Back at Erma's spring training camp, the players nicknamed one another. Erma Bergmann became "Bergie" professionally. The players stayed in dormitory-style accommodations during the two-week spring training.

When the All-American Girls Professional Baseball League made its debut in 1943, there were four teams: the South Bend Blue Sox, the Rockford Peaches, the Racine Belles and the Kenosha Comets. The next year, Milwaukee and Minneapolis teams brought the total to six. These latter two teams were moved and became the Grand Rapids Chicks and the Fort Wayne Daisies, respectively. Fans paid $1.40 to sit in box seats and $0.95 for the grandstand, and children were admitted for $0.30.

When Erma joined the crowd, it was an eight-team league with the addition of Peoria and Muskegon. Teams hailed from four midwestern states: Wisconsin, Michigan, Illinois and Indiana.

Erma launched her career with an appointment to the Muskegon Lassies. She wore the number 15 on the back of her shirt.

She tried out at third base and the outfield, positions she had played on the softball field. But her strong right arm propelled her to the pitcher's mound.

The Muskegon Lassies won the pennant in 1947. Erma is standing third from the right in this picture of the team. *Courtesy Erma Bergmann.*

Ralph "Buzz" Boyle, former Brooklyn Dodgers outfielder who coached Michigan's Muskegon Lassies, recognized Erma's pitching potential and took her under his wing.

Some sixty years later, Erma signed autographs at a baseball card show in St. Louis. After the show, she and her entourage stopped at a Goodwill store to shop. A customer recognized her AAGPBL shirt, her uniform for the autograph session. He asked her if she knew Buzz Boyle. "Yes," she exclaimed. "He was my manager in Muskegon."

"He was my grandfather," the fellow shopper said. The two baseball fans traded telephone numbers and met for dinner a couple of weeks later. Erma presented Buzz Boyle's grandson with a photograph of her and Buzz taken in Muskegon in 1946.

She explained how his grandfather changed her baseball career. Former softball pitchers found it difficult to adapt to the overhand pitching required in the new baseball league. Erma had never pitched softball, because she couldn't control the ball underhand. So she landed in the hot box, third base, or in the outfield. Her strong right arm played to her advantage in these positions. When Boyle, her manager, decided that she should try her hand at pitching, she didn't have to adjust to a new pitching style like former softball pitchers did.

Boyle instructed "Bergie" to move her arm up to knee level, and she mastered the submarine pitch. She clutched the ball on the seams, threw her left leg high in her windup and gradually raised her right arm to waist level. Soon she could hurl a pitch sidearm with full control of the ball. She was one of the first hurlers in the league to use the sidearm pitch, a style that bewildered many batters. She was heading for shoulder level and overhand pitching, but sidearm was permitted, and she could get the ball over the plate. So she stayed with the crossfire sidearm pitch for her entire career.

"I never had a sore arm throwing sidearm," she remembered.

The game of baseball revolves around the pitcher, according to Larry Jansen, who pitched for the New York Giants from 1947 to 1954 and ended his career in 1956 with the Cincinnati Reds. He analyzed his baseball position in his 1997 book *The Craft of Pitching*. He describes pitching as an art, a science and a craft. "From atop this 12-inch hill of dirt (the pitcher's mound), the ball is put into play. How this play develops resides largely in the arm, hands, and mind of the pitcher," Jansen writes.

Erma considered herself equal to the task.

Life was changing for her almost as fast as a race car on the Indianapolis Motor Speedway. By the end of spring training, her sidearm pumped the ball across the plate. The coaches divided the players according to talent to evenly balance the teams. The aim was keen competition and games that would keep the fans on the edges of their wooden bleachers.

ERMA M. BERGMANN
Uniform #15
Pitcher – H.O.F. 11-5-88

NO HITTER – 05-22-1947

Muskegon Lassies..... 1946-47
Springfield Sallies..... 1948
Racine Belles........... 1949-50
Battle Creek Belles.... 1951

The Muskegon Lassies climbed on a bus and traveled north from Pascagoula, playing exhibition games with the Racine Belles in Meridian and Jackson, Mississippi, and in Memphis and Chattanooga, Tennessee. Local charities benefited from the proceeds of these games, and fans were introduced to women's professional baseball. Erma and the Lassies spent their nights at hotels in these cities. Erma felt like an explorer discovering a new world.

This picture promoted the All-American Girls Professional Baseball League. *Courtesy Erma Bergmann.*

After the spring tour, the Lassies settled in Muskegon in time to tune up before the opening pitch of the 1946 season.

In the 1940s, the buses that transported the women's teams were rugged by today's standards. There was no bathroom on the bus. Sometimes, the vehicle's shocks were worn out, and the bus bounced along the highway. Erma found it impossible to sleep sitting on the bus, even after pitching a night game and traveling late at night. When the team arrived at their destination, Erma was either ready to eat or ready for bed.

Their daily schedule was sometimes grueling. They'd play a night game, shower, eat and board the bus as late as midnight. They might have a two-hundred-mile trip to the next town, arriving at two or three o'clock in the morning. The next morning, the players worked out and practiced for three or four hours until noon. In their free afternoons, they often did radio interviews. At five o'clock, it was time for more practice leading up to game time.

The players' own entertainment helped pass the time on the long bus trips. Charlene Pryor, center fielder for the Lassies, had served in the U.S. Marine Corps with Dick Jurgens during the war. She sang in the theatrical shows Jurgens and his band produced for the troops. The vocalist lifted spirits on the team bus by singing. Soon, all the girls were joining in the chorus. World War II songs like "I'll Get By" and "You'd Be So Nice to Come Home To" rang through the bus. Mary Rudis, who played for the Springfield Sallies, livened the bus party with her lowdown rendition of "A Good Man Is Hard to Find" and "St. Louis Blues."

Another song ranked at the top of the charts on the team buses. "The Victory Song." The official anthem of the ladies' league was written by two players, Lavonne "Pepper" Paire Davis and Nalda "Bird" Phillips.

Lavonne Davis played in the league from 1944 to 1953 with the Milwaukee Millerettes, the Racine Belles, the Fort Wayne Daisies and the Grand Rapids Chicks. She was a technical advisor for the movie *A League of Their Own*. During her career, she played hard. Six broken fingers and a broken collarbone were among her baseball souvenirs.

"Pepper" Davis was eighty-seven years old in March 2012 when she attended the twenty-fourth annual Joe DiMaggio Game at Fort Lauderdale Stadium. A photographer snapped her picture shaking hands with umpire Matt Hudson of Naples, Florida. The photo caption credited her as a "Legendary Lady" who inspired the movie *A League of Their Own*. Davis's baseball cap was perched on her head. She sat in a wheelchair, her cane hooked over the arm of the chair. Oxygen flowed through plastic tubing into her nose. Old age may have taken its toll on her once athletic body, but it failed to make a dent in her spirit.

Pepper Davis passed away in January 2013 at age eighty-eight. Some of her teammates and some of the actresses attended her funeral. They placed signed baseballs in her casket and sang the league song in her honor.

Nalda Phillips, the other member of the singing duo, learned to play baseball from her three brothers while growing up in Los Angeles. At age seventeen, she was invited to join the league's 1945 spring training at Wrigley Field. She was a hard-throwing left hander assigned to the South Bend Blue Sox.

"The Victory Song" still rings out at player reunions. The song these two ball players wrote goes like this:

Batter up!
Hear that call.
The time has come for one and all, to play ball.

For we're the members of the All-American League.
We come from cities near and far.
We've got Canadians, Irishmen and Swedes.

We're all for one,
We're one for all,
We're All-Americans!

Each girl stands, her head so proudly high,
Her motto "Do or die"
She's not the one to need or use an alibi.

Our chaperones are not too soft,
They're not too tough.
Our managers are on the ball.
We've got a president who really knows his stuff.

We're all for one,
We're one for all,
We're All-Americans!

The chaperones mentioned in the song were substitute mothers and nurses. They were also positive influences on the young players. Each team had a chaperone, and she made sure all the players had places to stay on the road. Sometimes, she sat in the hotel lobby to be sure everyone was in by midnight, their curfew on the road.

One night on the road, Erma was approached by a man in the hotel lobby. He asked her to go to dinner. She didn't want to get in a car with this stranger, so they walked to a restaurant near the hotel. When they returned, he invited her to come to his room. She refused and later learned he was a married man.

"Men come out at birth and spend the rest of their lives trying to get back in," she says in her sometimes salty style, referring with disdain to husbands who cheat on their wives.

Chaperones assigned roommates, medicated strawberries with hydrogen peroxide when players slid into a base and listened to the wails of homesick ballplayers. Chaperones decided if an injury prevented a player from returning to the field. The manager deferred to the chaperone's judgment on injury matters.

Erma's wounds were minimal. Pitchers were instructed not to slide into a base. Their job was to stay in top pitching form. Erma was glad that sliding wasn't in her job description.

She did sprain her ankle one day and was scheduled to pitch that night. Her manager sprayed her ankle to freeze it so she wouldn't feel the pain. Even though she felt no pain, she was conscious of the numbness. Erma was worried she would strain it again, not be able to feel it and do more damage. "It bothered me mentally," she remembered. But she pitched the entire game in her usual competitive style. By the time she came up again in the pitching rotation, her ankle felt better.

Chaperones also kept the players on straight and narrow paths. During Philip Wrigley's involvement with the league, if a player had a bottle of liquor in her closet, she was immediately sent home.

"I was glad to be playing professional ball, so I wasn't tempted to get drunk or break the curfew. I was afraid I'd get sent home," Erma recalled. The curfew didn't apply when the team was in their hometown. The girls stayed in private homes, and they didn't abuse the privilege of their nice living quarters.

The chaperones were attractive women who resembled movie stars. They added to the atmosphere on the field. Erma thought they looked like WAVES (Women Accepted for Voluntary Emergency Service), dressed in their sharp uniforms.

Helen Hannah Campbell was Erma's chaperone when she pitched for the Muskegon Lassies. Sixty-three years later, the two were still in touch with each other, bound by the good memories of being part of the great American pastime. Helen was friendly, tall, attractive and a good mixer with the women, Erma remembered.

Helen said: "The girls were a good bunch of ballplayers. They were real athletes. We chaperones were surrogate mothers to them.

My father was in professional baseball for thirty years," Helen said in a telephone interview from her retirement home in Fountain Valley, California. James Harrison "Truck" Hannah played on, coached and managed baseball teams. James took his only child along, and she met Joe DiMaggio, Ty Cobb and Lou Gehrig.

"My father was a catcher, and he played with Babe Ruth. That's how I got tangled up in baseball," said James's daughter, ninety-six years old at the time of the telephone interview.

The year before Erma joined the AAGPBL, players' charm school was discontinued. So part of the chaperone's job, according to Helen, was to make ladies out of the players. "We also arranged housing, made sure the uniforms were ready, got the paychecks, and arranged the buses. We were surrogate mothers. But the players really accepted me more like a buddy. If they wanted to go out and get a burger and a beer, I'd go with them," the chaperone remembered.

Shirley Burkovich, sixteen years old when she left Pittsburgh to become a Muskegon Lassie, described Helen Hannah's interrogation of a prospective date:

> After a game, this young boy asked me to go to the movies and I said, "We'll have to get permission." He said, "Well, okay." So, I went to Helen, and she said, "Well, I'll have to see him." So I told him, "You'll have to meet the chaperone." He kind of smiled and said, "Okay." He went in and came out, and this time he was laughing, and he said to me, "I didn't want to marry you. I just wanted to take you to the movies."

Eunice Kensler, a widow, had been a chaperone at spring training in Pascagoula, Mississippi. She was an older lady who retired at the end of the 1946 spring training. Kensler was well-to-do. Her husband had owned a drugstore in Florida. She returned to her home in Muskegon, Michigan, and asked Erma if she'd like to rent one of her bedrooms. Erma considered herself very fortunate to move into Mrs. Kensler's lovely two-story home.

In the meantime, Helen Hannah's father had introduced Helen to Max Carey, then president of the women's league, and he asked her to apply to be a chaperone. She joined the teams at spring training held in Havana, Cuba, in 1947 and was assigned to the Muskegon Lassies. Helen Hannah moved into Eunice Kensler's home with Erma.

Helen remembers Erma as being "a pretty good pitcher. She was a nice girl and she was competitive. She had a sense of humor that didn't quit." Helen continued, "Erma had an interesting, giggly laugh that I still remember."

Helen Hannah Campbell hails from Whittier, California, but her passport is stamped with Australia, Italy, Bangkok, Tahiti and the Yucatan. She was a classmate of Richard Nixon at Whittier Union High School and, in later years, was a docent at the Richard Nixon Library and Birthplace in Yorba Linda, California. She graduated from Woodbury College with a bachelor's degree in secretarial science and a minor in journalism and then went to work in a defense plant.

In 1943, she enlisted in the U.S. Marine Corps.

> *The Marines was the last branch of service to take women, because the commandant didn't want skirts with his male marines. But we showed them. For the ladies that followed, they have so much more than we had. Today, they have 225 job possibilities. We had only 30. Back then you couldn't be married or be pregnant. Now they have child care centers all over the place and encourage married women and men to stay on the base. Now that I look back on it, we went down the path first and opened up a lot of doors to young women who came behind us.*

After Helen's tour of active duty expired, she joined the Marine Corps Reserves in 1946.

When the Korean War began, she was recalled to active duty. She retired as a master gunnery sergeant after a thirty-two-year Marine Corps career that ended in 1975. Along the way, she lost two husbands, one in the Korean War and one in Vietnam. "Neither husband was a Marine, but I don't hold that against them," she quipped.

Helen stayed close to the Marine Corps by volunteering for them in her retirement. Parasailing and hot-air ballooning were some of her leisure pursuits. She also volunteered with the police department, patrolling Fountain Valley, California, where she lived in her later life. Helen passed away on March 24, 2013. She is thought to have been the last of the chaperones.

ERMA WALKED TO THE mound in her debut season as a professional baseball player, chomping on Wrigley chewing gum. She was a good advertisement for the league owner's product, taking out her tension on the juicy gum.

She heard the strains of "The Star-Spangled Banner," and the two teams stood in straight lines, forming a *V* for victory that met at home plate. World War II had ended the year before, and pride and patriotism ran rampant in the United States. Philip Wrigley encouraged patriotism and felt it would contribute to the league's success. Love of her country was part of Erma's core.

She stepped onto the pitching mound. Her eyes swept over the fans. Erma's right hand gripped the baseball, her fingers stroked the

Erma is in her Muskegon uniform, ready to step on the pitching mound. *Courtesy Erma Bergmann.*

seams. Her best pitches were a fastball and an inshoot, now called a curveball or cutter. With the snap of her wrist, her inshoot pitch traveled straight toward the middle of the plate, then drifted in on the batter's hands. Since Bergie was a right-handed pitcher, her curveball veered in on a left-handed batter and swayed away on a right-handed hitter. Today's cutter cuts to the left or to the right. In her rookie season, Erma's team won forty-six games and lost sixty-six.

There were several pitchers on the Muskegon team, so Bergie pitched every three or four days. She loosened up and worked out on her off days and sat on the bench during the games. The players called sitting on the bench "riding the pine." In those days, pitchers played the entire game. These girls were no sissies.

The season's schedule was grueling. The teams played 120 games a season, playing six nights a week with a doubleheader every Sunday. Fans came after church dressed in their Sunday best. "Sometimes I hoped for rain," Erma confided, remembering the demanding schedule, especially the doubleheaders.

For doubleheaders, the first game was nine innings and the second contest was seven innings. After the doubleheader, the players would shower, go out to eat and sometimes hop on the bus to head to the next city on their schedule.

Erma was serious about her baseball career. After all, this was a great job with a hefty paycheck. She wanted to be sure she kept it. The other players voiced the same intentions. Testimony to their seriousness was a game in a closely fought best-of seven series for the league championship in 1946 between the Racine Belles and the Rockford Peaches. The fourteen-inning game was played at Horlick Athletic Field in Racine, Wisconsin, before more than five thousand fans. With no score going into the fourteenth inning, Sophie Kurys, base-stealing champion of the league with 1,114 swiped bases from 1943 to 1952, singled, then promptly stole second base. When shortstop Moe Trezza drove a sharp ground ball into right field, Kurys raced around third and slid into home.

"They tried taping sliding pads to my legs," Sophie told the *Sports Illustrated* interviewer. "But they were so cumbersome. I told them, no, I'd just get the strawberries. Besides, the pads made it look as if my slip was showing."

The Racine Belles won the game, 1–0, and took the championship. Max Carey, who had played in the major leagues for twenty years, claimed at the end of the contest that it was the greatest baseball game he had ever seen.

This playoff game announced to the sports world that these women were competitive and serious about baseball. They didn't quit until there was a winner. What started as a means to satisfy baseball fans during World War II had taken on a life of its own.

Erma, too, had taken on a new life, and she enjoyed the camaraderie of her teammates and the opposing players. There were no disagreements or cattiness that Erma remembers. The girls were bound together like sisters by their love of playing baseball, their affection for one another and their unusual lifestyle for the 1940s. Erma recalled: "I loved the game. I loved everything about it. I loved the traveling, I loved the people I met. I never have had a bad memory about playing ball. Everything was above what I expected and above what I had. It was a pinnacle for a lot of us girls. It was a big thrill."

Erma produced a deck of plastic-coated Duratone playing cards. Each of the rust-colored cards had "EMB" printed in gold script on their fronts. The deck of cards slid into a felt cover that has protected them for some seventy years. She then exhibited a book of matches with her smiling face printed on the cover.

Erma stayed at Lookout Mountain Hotel when she played an exhibition game in Knoxville, Tennessee. The hotel overlooked seven states, she said. She saw how paper is made from tree pulp. She went to St. Augustine, Florida, and saw fish and turtles through the glass bottom of a boat. She sailed across the lake in Muskegon in a $10,000 motor-driven sailboat, a far cry from her South Broadway upbringing. The chef on board taught her how to prepare scalloped potatoes. Erma remembers his tall white chef's hat, the first she had ever seen.

Erma played golf at a country club in Muskegon and was paired with the club's professional golfer. After their round, the pro told her, "In five years you could be a professional golfer because of your natural ability."

"How can I play baseball and practice golf at the same time?" she asked. "I've got enough to do to play ball."

Her brothers visited her in Muskegon, and they all went for a ride in Mr. Brown's cabin cruiser. Mr. Brown owned the team. "Watching those women play was sensational," Otto remarked some sixty years later.

When the Muskegon Lassies played in Peoria, brothers Otto and Victor drove their parents to the game. This was the first time Erma's mother saw her play ball. And what an introduction she had! Erma hit a home run in the ninth inning and won the game for the Muskegon Lassies, 2–1.

After the game, Erma's parents and brothers stepped onto the field to congratulate their pitcher. Erma asked her mother if she knew how the game was played. Mother Sophie replied: "Yes. You stand out there and throw the ball for a while, and the other team swings the bat. Then the other team goes out and throws the ball for a while, and you swing the bat."

"That's the general idea, Mom," Erma acknowledged. "But sometimes I'm out in the field throwing the ball longer than they are."

Erma mentioned introspectively years later: "Your parents don't have to watch you play all the time. My parents only came twice in my fifteen years of playing, but I knew I had their unconditional support. People today think the parents have to be there all the time. I don't think that's true."

During a game in Peoria, the team raffled a car. About nine thousand people poured onto the field. This was the only time the league used a gimmick to attract fans. It really didn't need gimmicks. Fans pushed through the turnstiles because the games were highly competitive and the teams played sharp ball.

Baseball was not the only occupation opened up for women during World War II.

News of the Japanese attack on Pearl Harbor reached St. Louis at 1:31 p.m. on Sunday, December 7, 1941. The outbreak of war threw women into jobs they had never imagined performing. The shortage of men in the workforce opened up new positions for women. The "Rosie the Riveter" movement, which brought women into factories to support the war effort, boosted the number of working women to twenty million. The Rosies did more than build bombs. They carved out new roles for American women and changed the face of the workplace forever.

Ladies untied their aprons, pushed back from their desks, resigned as waitresses and sales clerks and became welders, crane operators and builders of tanks, B-29 bombers and lifeboats for battleships.

According to *Solidarity*, a magazine for United Auto Workers (UAW) members, Rosie the Riveters became heroes in hairnets. Erma's life had been spent pioneering uncharted courses, so it was natural for her to be one of the women who placed rivets in the fuselage of airplanes. She worked at McDonnell Douglas Aircraft Corporation in St. Louis one year during the baseball offseason.

"The company paid you a regular salary, sent you to school and gave you a toolbox. It was a great job," Erma said in an interview for the July/August 2004 issue of *Solidarity*. "All the rivets were inspected twice. If they didn't check out, they were marked with an 'X.' Then they were drilled out and done again. I found out why airplanes cost millions of dollars to make."

Erma had a variety of jobs. From December 1943 to August 1945, she was a painter at the Monsanto plant on Second Street behind her family's house. She painted the trim and sometimes dripped oil paint in her auburn hair and down her cheeks. She climbed on girders to paint the iron, balancing like a ballet dancer. She worked side by side with men. She earned one dollar an hour. She worked six days a week and collected forty-eight dollars each week, an exceptional salary for a nineteen-year-old woman. With that kind of income, she and another young woman painted the town red in their off-hours. When she left to play ball, Mr. Gillman, her supervisor, told her she could come back anytime.

She also inspected bullets at a McQuay Norris plant during World War II. She kept her pitching arm in shape at a bowling alley.

She spent the winters of 1946 and 1947 packing saccharin to be exported to China. The artificial sweetener is five hundred times sweeter than sugar, according to Erma.

Erma was a regular customer at Jack's Barbeque on Highway 66 outside of St. Louis. She was home for the winter, and the restaurant owner asked her if she would like to wait tables. Erma was hesitant, since she had never done that kind of work. He assured her she could do it, so she accepted the job. Her salary was forty dollars a week, the union wage at that time, and she earned twenty dollars in tips. She frowns when she remembers the customer who tipped her one penny. She worked at Jack's for one week to prove to herself she could be a waitress.

Erma not only accepted challenges, she also looked for them. She's in the same pioneer class as Sally Ride, the first American woman in space. As a youngster, Sally played baseball and football with the neighborhood boys. Her dream was to be a professional tennis player. She changed course and studied physics, earning a doctorate in astrophysics. When NASA advertised for astronauts, there were eight thousand applicants, one thousand of them women. Sally always felt privileged to have been chosen. Both Erma's and Sally's families encouraged their daughters to be what they wanted to be.

When Erma came home in September after her first season, she bought a $100 Hamilton watch. She also wanted to buy a used car. She had her eye on a Plymouth that cost $1,200. She had saved $700. Banks refused to lend her the $500 difference, since she did not have a year-round job.

She approached Mr. Mecklenberg, who owned the cigar store with the wooden Indian outside. He was a kind bachelor and lent her the $500. He said, "You come from a good family." There was no note signed. The transaction was cemented with a handshake. Erma repaid him and bought him a white dress shirt to thank him for his favor.

Her second season as a professional baseball player was an adventure, from spring training to the playoff games.

6

HUSTLING TO HAVANA

I bought a bottle of rum at a distillery.
I thought I would keep it for a special occasion. I still have it.
—Erma Bergmann

Baseball is Cuba's national pastime. So it seemed only natural for 150 All-American Girls players to board a plane at the Miami airport and fly across the Straits of Florida to Havana, Cuba, for spring training in 1947.

That year was a milestone in baseball history as well as in the civil rights movement, because Jackie Robinson broke the racial barrier. Branch Rickey, owner of the Dodgers, hired him as a first baseman, and Robinson became the first African American to play in the major leagues. He was named Rookie of the Year.

In Havana, the women's games attracted great crowds of spectators. The All-Americans "became the rage of all baseball-mad Cuba," according to the official account of the league's 1947 pre-season. "Hundreds turned out to see them practice. And no less than 55,000 wildly enthusiastic fans watched the round-robin tournament, four exhibition games, which concluded the training program." Helen Hannah, the Lassies chaperone who would become Erma's mentor, was in charge of all the chaperones at spring training.

Grantland Rice MovieTone News filmed Erma's pitching for its newscast, shown daily in movie theaters throughout the United States. She stood on the mound, sunglasses perched on her nose, and fired the ball over the plate while the movie camera whirred.

For Erma, the thought of traveling outside the United States or visiting an island never entered her mind. But here she was in Cuba's glamorous capital city. Havana was the island playground for America's rich and famous. The city flaunted its decadence with casinos, large hotels, prostitutes, nightclubs, big cigars and fine rum. The Cuban coffee was served in demitasse cups. Erma thought that drinking the strong coffee was like drinking the juice of the coffee bean.

Ernest Hemingway tipped Papa Dobles (giant daiquiris) at Havana's Floridita bar while entertaining Hollywood's Spencer Tracy and Ava Gardner. He found Havana an ideal place for fishing and for writing.

Erma and her teammates stayed at the Seville Biltmore Hotel, with its sumptuous tile lobby. The Seville Biltmore was the fanciest hostelry Erma had ever seen. She mailed her mother a picture postcard of the hotel. Part of her message read: "We are really doing some heavy practice but feel fine. Just a little sore. I really like our manager Bill Wamby."

Other Cuban hotels were fine, too. The Hotel Plaza had a rooftop bar. The most elegant of all was the Hotel Nacional, built in 1930.

The girls were instructed to go out in groups of four or five, not alone or in pairs. The chaperones must have worked and worried overtime. Erma remembered seeing what she thought were prostitutes climb a stairway to their place of business.

The ballplayers were forbidden to drink the Cuban water. Some of the players took salt tablets to cope with the heat, but Erma did not. She was also able to tolerate the Cuban diet.

May 1 is International Workers Day, a holiday in Cuba. The players found that almost everything was closed. Cubans gathered in the streets to celebrate. There was some unrest in the country and fear that violence might occur. The girls were restricted to their hotel for safety. They resumed spring training the next day.

"I wasn't afraid," said Erma, who was twenty-three at the time. "We were taken on a tour of a distillery and sat on barrel seats. We had samples of rum. I bought a bottle to keep for a special occasion. I thought if I got married, we could celebrate with this bottle of rum direct from Cuba. I still have the bottle," she said. Eighty-eight-year-old Erma laughed when she told this story.

Doris "Sammye" Sams of Knoxville, Tennessee, trained with Erma in Havana. They were teammates and fellow pitchers in Muskegon in 1947, the year the Lassies won the pennant.

"Erma was a good pitcher and she could hit the ball. She was real nice, too," remembered Doris. This was a noteworthy evaluation from Erma's peer, who was Most Valuable Player in 1947 and 1949. Only Doris Sams and one other player were MVPs two years. She was a five-time All-Star during her eight-year career, which ended in 1953. Her crowning glory was her induction into the National Women's Baseball Hall of Fame in October 2012 in Chevy Chase, Maryland. She is one of only thirty-seven current and former players in women's regulation baseball inducted since 1998.

Unfortunately, Sammye didn't live long enough to witness her induction. When Sams died in June 2012 at age eighty-eight, the *New York Times* lauded her league-record 12 home runs in 1952 and her batting average above .300 in each of her last four seasons. The newspaper recalled that she once outdueled Lois Florreich of the Rockford Peaches through twenty-two innings, winning, 1–0, in a game that had been tied after the scheduled seven innings of the short game of a doubleheader.

"After that, I told my manager, 'I don't want to pitch any more seven-inning games. They're too long.'" Sue Macy quoted Sams in her league history, *A Whole New Ball Game*.

"Sammye" was pitcher perfect in a game for Muskegon, not allowing anyone to reach first base. "The game was getting along, and no one had reached base," Sammye remembered in a telephone conversation from Knoxville. "A batter came up to the plate, and I knew she was going to knock it. She hit the ball, it hit my knee, almost tore off my kneecap and ricocheted to the shortstop, who threw her out at first base. That shortstop saved my perfect game. Pitchers can't do it all. It takes a whole team."

"It seemed like about 120 degrees during spring training in Cuba. I took salt tablets. We did have a lot of people come to the games. We made a lot of money down there," said Sams.

Cuba's Tropicana nightclub and casino opened its doors in a leafy Havana garden on December 30, 1939. About the time the All-American Girls arrived in Cuba, big-name talent and voluptuous cabaret girls known as "Goddesses of the Flesh" graced the Tropicana's stage. Liberace, Nat King Cole and Carmen Miranda were among the performers. Xavier Cugat and his band, Josephine Baker and Cuban star Celia Cruz were also headliners at the Tropicana. Many nights, the audience was just as famous. Marlon Brando, Sammy Davis Jr. and Greta Garbo were spotted watching the floor show. Havana was Hollywood and Las Vegas rolled into one.

During Prohibition in the United States, which began in 1920 and ended in 1933, ships traveled ninety miles back and forth between Key West and Havana, where liquor was legal.

Colonel Fulgencio Batista seized power in 1934 and ruled Cuba until he was forced to flee the country on New Year's Eve 1958. History records this as a time of graft and corruption in public office. Revolutions simmered, and unrest rumbled through the island. It's reported that an incident occurred while the All-American Girls were there. Player Thelda Marshall recalled a two-day uprising when "we couldn't leave the hotel. We had to lower buckets so they could send us up Cokes."

Fidel Castro was a law student at the University of Havana the year the women practiced in Cuba. Castro led his Cuban revolution in 1959 and took over the government. When the Cuban Communist Party was established in 1965, Castro became its leader. He held that position until 2011, when illness forced him to relinquish his responsibilities to his brother Raúl Castro.

Near the end of spring training, the American ballplayers participated in an exhibition game against the Cuban women's team. More than twenty thousand spectators jammed the stands to watch and cheer.

Fourteen-year-old Isabel "Lefty" Alvarez's mother signed for her talented, athletic daughter and sent her to America to play professional ball. Her mother saw this as the road out of poverty for Isabel. And indeed it was. By this time, there were players from the United States, Canada and Cuba in the girls' league.

This adventure in Cuba lasted one glorious week, and the season was about to begin. The teams traveled to their home cities, and umpires across the Midwest shouted, "Play ball!"

Erma and the Muskegon Lassies took the field under the direction of manager Bill Wambsganss, better known as Wamby. Wamby had a claim to fame, one that had caused the baseball world to take notice in 1921. "He executed the only unassisted triple play in World Series history," Erma said. He covered second base for the Cleveland Indians in the 1921 World Series against the Brooklyn Dodgers. In the fifth inning of the fifth game, Wamby caught a line drive, forced a runner on his way to third and tagged the runner approaching from first base.

He played in the major leagues from 1914 to 1926 with the Cleveland Indians, the Boston Red Sox and the Philadelphia Athletics. Wamby's players and associates liked and respected him. He told his female athletes, "When you play in the big league, you should know what to do with the ball when it's hit to you."

He led his band of spirited and competitive lady baseball players to win the pennant in 1947, Muskegon's rookie season. He is the manager who stands out in Erma's memory more than half a century later.

She, no doubt, stood out in his memory, too, because of one particular highlight of her baseball career. The *Grand Rapids Herald* recorded the game with a screaming headline: "Bergmann Hurls No-Hitter, Beats Chicks 4–1!" A crowd of 1,621 attended the contest.

May 22, 1947, was a drizzly gray day. It was Erma's turn in the rotation to pitch. "I never liked to pitch when it was raining," Erma frowned.

She gripped the slippery baseball and fired it toward the plate. She retired the side, inning after inning. It was a pitchers' battle between Erma and Alice Haylett of the Grand Rapids Chicks. The rival pitchers hurled shutout ball for five innings. The players' muscles tightened. Their eyes followed the pitchers' balls from the mound to the plate. Erma held her breath when the bat connected with the ball. But Erma's defense backed her up, and still no Chick got a hit.

In the sixth inning, Erma's team scored two runs. As the game slipped into the late innings, the pressure and excitement mounted. Erma was on her way to pitching a no-hitter.

The Grand Rapids Chicks scored one run, thanks to the rain that continued to pelt the field. It was the seventh inning when Chick Dottie Stolze hit a grounder that skidded off the second sacker's glove for a two-base error. Erma grimaced when the next batter hit a roller to the shortstop and the wet ball again slipped away. The errors let the Chicks score the only run. But there were still no hits.

Erma helped her own cause in the seventh inning with a single. This was followed up by a walk, and then a teammate banged another single, scoring a run. In the eighth inning, Lenard, a Lassie, singled, went to second on McGuire's walk, took third on Fischer's single and scored on a squeeze bunt.

After nine innings, Erma had pitched a no-hitter, and the Muskegon Lassies won the game, 4–1. Her teammates clapped her on the back and shared the excitement of her accomplishment.

Erma's earned run average for that season was an impressive 1.74, with 11 wins and 10 losses. The *Muskegon Chronicle* called Erma the "submarine ball star."

"Erma's pitching was real good for us," Doris Sams recalled. "There was no sense of competition among the pitchers." The five-foot, nine-inch Doris switched to the outfield and was delighted that she could play every day. She remembered Erma's cheering everybody on and yelling all the time if she wasn't pitching.

"Sammye" hailed from Knoxville, Tennessee, and lived her whole life in the family home. She entered the league through a notice in the local newspaper. She tried out, and the officials immediately said: "Go home and get some clothes. You're going to be a ball player." Her father, who had started her playing ball and batting at age three or four, wanted her to go. But her mother was hesitant. She knew her daughter wanted to do it.

Sams played eight years, retiring in 1953. She returned to Knoxville and got a job with the electric company working with computers. She retired from there after twenty-five years to take care of her mother, who died a couple of months after she retired. Then she played golf. "I haven't played lately," said the eighty-year-old, "I've gotten so puny."

Doris remembered a game when she was on first. The third-base coach signaled her to run, but she stayed at first base. After the game, he told her he was going to fine her for not following directions. She lifted her skirt and showed him a raw hip from sliding. "Oh, I forgot about that," he said. It takes a week or two for those injuries to heal. When men in the stands saw the girls slide to a base in their skirts, they said, "You couldn't pay me enough money to slide in those outfits."

One day during the 1947 season, Erma couldn't seem to get the ball over the plate, no matter how hard she tried. Dottie "Mickey" Maguire was Erma's catcher that year. The two players became good friends. But Erma's wild pitches this day dismayed and irritated Mickey.

The feisty Irish gal flipped her catcher's mask from her face, threw it on the ground and stalked to the mound. "Get the gosh darn ball over the plate," Mickey Maguire commanded.

"What do you think I'm doing? I'm trying to get it over the plate," Erma replied.

Rick Chapman, Mickey's son, recalled how tough his mother was on Erma and the other pitchers. "She would cuss and yell at Erma, then throw the ball back to the pitcher's mound faster than the pitch." he recalled recently. Rick became president of the Players Association many years later.

Erma never intentionally hit a batter with a pitch. But the ball accidentally grazed an opponent when they played in Kenosha. Catcher Maguire threw off her mask and sprinted to the pitcher's mound to protect and defend Erma in case a skirmish occurred. Mickey got there before anyone else.

Mickey always said that Erma threw a heavy ball when pitching, so heavy that Mickey had sponge in her glove to protect her hand. Erma's pitches had speed, and when they landed, you could hear the catcher's glove go off like a shotgun. She threw fastballs and curveballs. She didn't have much of a changeup (a pitch that changes speeds), because she had trouble getting that

How proud Erma was when she bought this 1951 Chevrolet convertible. *Courtesy Erma Bergmann.*

pitch over the plate. "It had to be over the plate. Nobody's going to swing at a pitch in the dirt," Erma admitted.

The Muskegon Lassies' 1947 yearbook, which cost twenty-five cents, described the fans from one of the games. A half-dozen women, fresh from their aprons, their faces still reflecting the heat of cooking ovens, argued the merits of the girls. At one side were a man and his wife who never missed a game. A disabled person hobbled in each night, feeling in the game the thrills of competition his nonfunctioning legs never would allow him to experience personally. Another group of housewives arrived earlier than other fans and sat in the same seats each evening. On the other side was a group of office girls and their boyfriends; they came to every game. "These are the new fans of America's new game," the yearbook reported. In 1946, ninety thousand fans paid to enter Marsh Field to see the Lassies play. The next year's attendance was expected to go well over one hundred thousand.

When the team won the 1947 pennant in a close race, the women were jubilant. Mr. Brown, the team's owner, took the players on a fancy picnic at the country club to celebrate. The women were also guests at luncheons given by the Lions and Kiwanis Clubs.

There was whooping and hollering in Muskegon, Michigan, even though the Lassies lost to the Racine Belles in the first round of the playoffs. But Erma and the pennant-winning Lassies were intoxicated with their triumph.

7

CRUISING TO THE BEACH

I actually cried when I heard I was traded.
—*Erma Bergmann*

Erma returned home for the winter with her most successful season under her belt. The next spring, she rode the train to Miami for spring training in Opa-locka, Florida, at a naval air base. All eight teams trained together in 1948. After that year, the teams trained individually at locations of their choosing.

Erma traveled to Florida in style, spending the night stretched out on the upper bunk in the Pullman car. She still remembered the thrill of that train trip.

She arrived at camp, glad to see her friends from Muskegon. Then she heard some bad news. She had been traded to the Springfield Sallies, an expansion team that needed veteran players. "I actually cried when I heard I was traded," Erma remembered. Tom Hanks, the manager in the movie *A League of Their Own*, announces to his team of girls, "There's no crying in baseball." But there was crying when Erma left her family of ballplayers, the girls she had lived with, eaten with and played ball with for two years. She was leaving the team of champions. She was especially miffed that no mention of her trade had been made to her beforehand. She was not notified until spring training began.

"Why didn't they tell me at the end of the previous season or before spring training? How could this happen?" she wondered. The Muskegon Lassies was the team she had helped to win the pennant. This was the team for whom she pitched a no-hitter. Erma was never a crybaby, but this was one of the few times in her life that she shed tears before moving on.

Despite her tears about being traded, Erma still loved the game. She still loved the adventure and the prestige that followed her the rest of her life. And she earned more money than she ever imagined she could. She dried her tears, picked up her Marty Marion glove and her spikes and joined the Springfield Sallies.

This was 1948, the year the *Chicago Daily Tribune* prematurely declared New York Governor Thomas E. Dewey winner in the presidential race over Harry S. Truman. President-elect Truman stood on the caboose of a train passing through St. Louis's Union Station, laughing as he held high a copy of the newspaper with the erroneous headline.

It was also the women's baseball league's most successful year. The games attracted almost one million fans. The women grew in reputation and notoriety as well. When Philadelphia Athletics manager Connie Mack saw shortstop Dottie Schroeder in action, he said, "If that girl were a man, she'd be worth $50,000 to me."

Former New York Yankees first baseman Wally Pipp classified Dorothy Kamenshek as "the fanciest-fielding first baseman I've ever seen." When Dottie died in May 2010 at age eighty-four in Palm Desert, California, the *New York Times* extolled her career with the Rockford Peaches from 1943 to 1951 and again in 1953. She finished among the league's top ten career batting leaders, with an average of .292. She was named one of the top one hundred female athletes of the century by *Sports Illustrated*, reported the *Times*. The television show *CBS Sunday Morning* paid tribute to the star first baseman.

Time magazine said Dottie was offered a contract with a men's minor league team, but she refused. Dottie retired from playing in 1953, graduated from Marquette University with a degree in physical therapy and became chief of the Los Angeles Crippled Children's Services Department. Success for "Kammie" wasn't limited to one field, commented *Time*.

Back in Springfield, Illinois, Erma's brothers visited her. "I was living with an old lady in her home. She was a super housekeeper. You could eat off her floors. She made my brothers take their shoes off before coming into the house." Erma resented her landlady's treatment of her brothers. "It hurt my feelings. The weather wasn't even bad. Most times there were two of us who stayed together in someone's home, but not this time. I decided if I came back to Springfield the next year, I would not stay with her. But I didn't go back."

The Springfield team was the worst in the league and was unable to draw crowds. After a year, the Sallies lost their home field and joined the Chicago Colleens as touring player development teams. The Sallies were gone for good by 1951.

Erma was happy to be traded to the Racine Belles. She had made friends with the team's players during their encounters with one another. The Racine Belles yearbook described Erma as sturdy and strong with an easy pitching delivery. "You get paid and you play wherever they send you," she explained. Erma had learned to accept change, whether she agreed with it or not. In 1949, spring training was held in West Baden, Indiana, the site of the exclusive resort West Baden Springs Hotel. At one time, a private train ran a couple of miles between West Baden and French Lick, Indiana, another elegant resort touting curative mineral baths.

Erma usually enjoyed living in different homes. The league checked the landlords before allowing their players to stay. In Racine, she stayed at the home of a man who worked for a hotel. The family was musical, and the parents and their four children spent the evenings singing around the piano. Erma lifted her voice in song and thoroughly enjoyed the entertainment.

When Erma played with the Racine team in 1949 and 1950, her chaperone was Mildred "Willie" Wilson, one of Erma's favorite people. Willie was an attractive sports star in her own right. She was a native of Brooklyn and a physical education graduate from Long Island University. She was manager and catcher for the New York Celtics Softball Team.

Willie moved to Racine for her new job with the Belles and enjoyed her career as chaperone, handling first aid, equipment, housing, traveling and deportment and morale for the team. She thought Erma's soulful eyes made her look like the popular 1940s movie star Ann Sheridan.

Willie was an outstanding basketball player and had been a New York model, according to Erma's memory. She and her business partner, Joann Winter, owned a candy and confections store in the lobby of the Racine Hotel. Mildred later married a doctor and had one daughter, Erma said.

When the Racine team folded, Erma pitched her way into Battle Creek, Michigan. It was 1951, her last year with the All-American Girls Professional Baseball League. She got a raise, from $75.00 to $85.00 a week. She not only played but also was appointed chaperone, earning an extra $50.00 per week. As chaperone, Erma sent the uniforms to the cleaners, doled out the $3.50 meal money on the road, administered first aid and arranged roommates at the hotels.

Erma bought a used black Chevrolet convertible with a gleaming white top and a red and gray interior. Erma worked hard for her money, and she knew how to enjoy it.

While playing with the Battle Creek Belles, she visited the Kellogg's factory and saw Corn Flakes baking to a golden brown in enormous ovens. She saw Brunswick pool tables and bowling balls being made. Erma found the league to be a great education and a stepping stone in her life. Fame and fortune went hand in hand in the AAGPBL.

But times were changing. Attendance at the women's games began to falter. Their best year had been 1948, when ten teams drew almost 911,000 fans, an impressive increase from the 176,000 onlookers who had showed up in 1943. Their publicity and promotion budget was $8,445 in 1948. The next year, two teams were dropped, and only $3,341 was spent for promotion. Attendance was cut almost in half.

The September 1950 issue of *McCall's* praised the women's game and mentioned that nearly one million spectators bought tickets in 1948, more than half of them women. Many men were fans, too, according to the article. After gawking at the players' bare knees and legs for an inning, the male fans watched in wonderment at the skill of the fielders, the lusty swings of the batters and the assortment of stuff the pitchers served. The article also mentioned Lib Mahon, a teacher in the offseason who used her baseball earnings to pay for a master's degree. The writer declared the game great for players and fans, but especially for the athletes. "The opportunity to show that you are good at something," Morris Markey wrote, "to have people yell their approval of you injects powerful ingredients into the soul."

This display of approval must have stuck in Erma's soul the rest of her life. She always played to win.

Erma was twenty-six years old when she came home for a visit. Her nineteen-year-old brother, Victor, wanted to borrow about $250 from her for a Harley motorcycle. Mother Bergmann was opposed to the idea, fearful that Victor would get hurt on the cycle. Erma had always been a soft touch when it comes to buying anything for her family, especially Victor and later his three children. She gave her brother the money, and he cruised away on his motorcycle.

Soon after, the telephone rang in the Bergmann house. Erma was home to answer it. It was a nurse at City Hospital, notifying the family that Victor had crashed his motorcycle into a concrete lamppost and lay in a coma. Although Erma couldn't bear to go to the scene of the accident, a friend told her that one of her brother's blond curls was stuck to the post.

Erma and her mother rushed to the hospital, and her mother fainted when she saw her unconscious son, his wrapped head lying motionless on the pillow. Victor was in a coma for ten days. Erma spent those ten days fearful that Victor wouldn't live. "If something had happened to him, I would never have forgiven myself for giving him the money to buy the motorcycle. The accident would have been my fault," she lamented.

Victor did recover, much to Erma's relief. She then returned to her baseball career.

Erma played for the Battle Creek Belles in 1951, her last year with the league. Her salary swelled to $90 per week with the addition of $50 in transportation money for spring training in Florida. On her arrival, she was awarded $25, and she received the other $25 at the end of the Florida season.

Her career earned-run average for her six years with the All-American Girls Professional Baseball League was an impressive 2.56. She could foresee the demise of the league and felt it was going into extra innings. Revenue declined. Few new players emerged.

Servicemen had returned from the war and displaced women in factories. Women were no longer needed to make guns, ammunition and airplanes. Women were relegated to low-paying jobs and had to return to traditional female occupations such as waiting tables in restaurants. Male ballplayers returned to the diamond, and fans paid to watch men, instead of women, play major league games.

Television was introduced to the public, and people pressed their noses against appliance store windows to watch this new phenomenon. Viewers were mesmerized by this revolutionary form of entertainment. Gradually, television sets with small black-and-white screens showed up in living rooms. Neighborhood children gathered in dark houses, sprawled on floors. A dim light flickered from the television screen, keeping the living room from total darkness. The young guests came to watch Milton Berle, "Uncle Miltie" in his *Texaco Star Theater*, as well as Hopalong Cassidy and Lucille Ball. This new in-home entertainment played a part in the demise of the AAGPBL. The league folded in 1954.

Although the world around her was different from when she left home to play ball, Erma and the daring women who were part of the All-American Girls Professional Baseball League had carved their niche in sports history. The one-third of the original six hundred players who are still alive are revered by sports fans across the country. They were idols and role models in their day, too.

Bill Veeck sold the Cleveland Indians and bought the St. Louis Browns baseball team in 1951. Veeck was a master at creating gimmicks to attract fans to Browns games. The team was poor, but the sideshows were a hit. Veeck thought if a female professional baseball player pitched to a midget while a one-arm outfielder covered the outfield, the threesome would get people through the turnstiles and into the ballpark.

He recruited Erma to pitch to Eddie Gaedel. Eddie, who stood three feet, seven inches tall, had one historic at bat with the Browns on August 19, 1951. He walked on four pitches and was lifted for a pinch runner, but he became an instant legend.

Pete Gray was a one-arm outfielder. He played for the Browns in 1945, his only year in the major leagues. He lost his arm while working on his family's farm in Pennsylvania when he slipped off the running board of his father's pickup truck. The truck ran over his right arm. A few days later, his arm was amputated. His dream had always been to play Major League Baseball. He may have lost his arm, but he did not lose his dream.

He learned to throw with his left hand and bat one-handed. He learned to field the ball in his glove and pitch the ball in the air while he tucked his glove under his stump of an arm. He caught the ball with his bare hand and fired it into the infield. His strong arm and athletic ability amazed players and fans alike, according to the St. Louis Browns Historical Society.

He was a semipro star in the coal towns of his native Pennsylvania. He entered professional baseball in 1942, garnering national attention when he batted .333 for Memphis in 1944. He hit 5 home runs, tied a league record by stealing 68 bases and was named the Southern Association's Most Valuable Player. This remarkable season earned Pete a shot with the Browns in 1945.

The year he played for the Browns, he was clearly overmatched at the major league level. Although his season with the team was lackluster, he was a wonder to watch, a study in agility and dexterity as an outfielder. He was also an inspiration to World War II veterans who had returned home missing limbs.

These were the players teamed up with Erma for this baseball entertainment. But the show never played to the crowd. Erma explained that Bill Veeck could not get insurance coverage on her, so he was not able to let her pitch. "I was disappointed," Erma said. "I was anxious to see if I could pitch to that little guy."

Erma wasn't quite ready to hang up her baseball glove. She heard about the formation of a women's winter league in Florida. Teams from Hollywood, Fort Lauderdale, Miami and Miami Beach would compete and

Erma was traded to the Racine Belles. She enjoyed the Wisconsin beach when she had time off from practicing ball. *Courtesy Erma Bergmann.*

entertain Floridians and tourists. The four-team league would play six nights a week. The players stayed in the Dorn Hotel Apartments in Miami for $10 a week. The league paid $25 for traveling expenses to Florida and allowed another $25 for the players' return home at the end of the season. Players also had the option of signing a new contract for the Chicago season when the Florida season ended.

Erma knew some of the players in the new league, so she packed her convertible and cruised to the Sunshine State. She pitched for the Miami Beach team, but the appeal of women playing professional baseball had waned. The women competed with dog races, horse races, jai alai and drinking, according to Erma. Jai alai (pronounced "hi lie") is touted as the fastest game on earth.

The women's baseball games in the 1950s did not draw spectators, and the Florida league folded in a month, almost as quickly as it began. Erma and two other players from the team rented an apartment and decided to stay another month or two. The girls piled in Erma's convertible every day and headed for the beach. Erma strolled the beach in a white Jansen bathing suit.

They were prepared for foamy waves lapping over the beach and sand fleas rollicking in the white grains, but they didn't expect the bite of the love bug. Both Erma and her roommate met gentlemen in Miami, and both enjoyed serious relationships. As a matter of fact, Erma's friend married the man she met that year in Miami and stayed in the Sunshine State.

Erma walked through a Miami hotel lobby and bumped into a good-looking professional football player and his friend from New York. Erma's evaluation of a man was partially based on his athletic prowess. "I liked athletic men, not wimps," Erma remarked. Mitch met Erma's high standards.

Mutual attraction pulled Mitch and Erma together like magnets. Erma was no stranger to romance. She had had plenty of dates. Some men came to the women's baseball games to flirt with the players while they signed autographs after the game.

Erma's first boyfriend was her Croatian catcher in the cinder lot on South Broadway. Erma was fifteen years old, and Pete Randick was about nineteen. All the boys in the old neighborhood dated her at some time or another.

Another beau was Frank Felder, a Jewish osteopath who had an office on South Broadway. He had a brilliant mind and loved learning. He told Erma, "I'd rather go to school all my life than work." True to his word, he returned to school and earned a law degree.

He took Erma bowling, and when his first ball rolled into the gutter, he flunked Erma's athletic test. "But I loved talking with him because I learned a lot," she remembered. "He told me, 'You've got more common sense than a lot of college graduates.'"

William Koons grew up in Erma's neighborhood and joined the U.S. Navy during World War II. Erma was nineteen, and twenty-two-year-old Bill was home from the service when they dated. Bill received two bad conduct citations, one for punching an officer. When Erma learned he was AWOL (absent without leave), she was suspicious. When the second bad conduct citation came around, Bill was discharged from the navy, and Erma backed out of their relationship.

Some friends introduced Erma to Mike Sporich, a handsome merchant marine. Mike was divorced and had a child. He wasn't ready to marry again, but he told Erma, "They don't make women like you anymore."

"The ones I liked, there was always something wrong as far as marrying them went. The ones I could marry, I didn't want to," Erma recalled. But Mitch was different. He made a lasting impression. Their courtship was as hot as the Florida sun.

Mitch Stempin had played for the Chicago Rockets, an American football team in the All-America Football Conference (AAFC), from 1946 to 1949. In Chicago, the National Football League's Chicago Bears and the Chicago

Mitch and Erma met in Miami Beach. They discussed marriage, but it never happened.
Courtesy Erma Bergmann.

Cardinals were well entrenched. The Rockets was not one of the three AAFC teams invited to join the National Football League prior to the 1950 season.

The three girls and two boys drove from Florida to Minnesota to go fishing. The uneven number was by design. They were traveling as a group, not in pairs, and the girls felt this ensured their safety.

When their vacations ended, Mitch persuaded Erma to move to Chicago, his hometown. Erma and another ballplayer and Mitch drove the convertible straight through from Miami to St. Louis, then on to Chicago. Erma could not be persuaded to spend a night in a motel with a man. So they kept driving. When they passed through St. Louis, Erma's mother cooked a German dinner for them, complete with her famous potato pancakes.

Life was good. Erma was in love.

8

SOUTH SIDE OF CHICAGO

He'll go a long way before he'll find a girl like you, Erma.
—Mrs. Conklin, Erma Bergmann's landlady

Love may have lured Erma to the Windy City, but she also knew about the National Girls Baseball League in Chicago. With the All-American League on the way out and the Florida women's teams already in the showers, Erma saw the move to Chicago as the chance to continue playing professional ball. She and her player friend, who was a native of the midwestern city, tried out and scored with the Chicago league.

Erma pitched for the Bluebirds in 1952, the year the team was the champion among the four teams. Then she joined the Chicago Queens, managed by Freda Savona, a tough female ballplayer. Under her tutelage, Erma made the news. She pitched a twenty-three-inning game and tied a league record. Some years later, she was asked if she grew tired pitching the long game. She said, "I was young then and it didn't bother me." She also hit five singles in five at bats, tying another record.

Erma's 1953 contract quoted a salary of $100 per week, a hefty raise. Her salary included making herself available for publicity pictures and radio interviews when requested by the league.

Mitch went back to his work driving a tow truck and wholesaling cars. Through an agency, Erma got a part-time job at Katz Wagner & Co., a law and accounting firm on the twenty-third floor of a building at 105 West Adams in Chicago's Loop. She was the keeper of the vault that held clients' wills. She answered the phone, and if a client inquired about his will, she retrieved it from the depths of the vault. Since Mitch was Catholic, Erma was beginning to think about joining his church. One of the secretaries at work agreed to be her witness if there was a wedding. She gave Erma a Catholic prayer book.

Erma made a trip home to visit her parents. Her father chastised her about her thinking of becoming Catholic. "Is someone trying to talk you into this?" he questioned. Then he didn't talk to her for the rest of her visit. She cried when she left to return to Chicago. Some weeks later, she was relieved to know her father's bitterness dissolved before Erma's next trip home.

Erma worked her office job in the morning until noon and then played ball three or four nights a week at Shrewbridge Field. She earned $250 a week from both jobs, enough to afford lunch at the Palmer House Hotel, one of Chicago's finest, where she ate fresh fish on Fridays.

The first year in Chicago, Erma and two other players rented a trailer. The next year, ten ballplayers rented the third floor of a mansion owned by Rocky DeGrazio, an old-time Chicago mobster. Erma took the Rock Island train from the suburb to the Loop for her office job. The large house had a bar in the basement. It was open to the renters and appeared to Erma to be a haven for fancily dressed call girls who came and went. Erma was exposed to another side of life. She learned to keep her mouth shut, a trait that served her well the rest of her life.

The ballplayers paid $250 a month for the penthouse, a bargain when divided among ten women. The large room on the third floor had three couches and double beds with plenty of space for the women who stayed there for a season. DeGrazio and his wife occupied the second floor of the house.

Erma and Mitch's romance blossomed. He picked her up from her games and took her to fine restaurants and theaters with stage shows. They also played the horses at Maywood Park and Hawthorne Race Course. When Erma's mother flew to Chicago to visit her, Mitch and Erma picked her up at the airport, and Mitch took them to the Stockyard Inn, an elite steak restaurant.

Erma was courted not only by Mitch, but by his mother, too. "You marry him. You get him," Mitch's mother encouraged in her Polish accent. But Erma was beginning to realize that Mitch was jealous and had a temper that flared like a Fourth of July rocket. But Erma was deeply in love.

In 1953, Erma rented a room upstairs in Mrs. Conklin's house. She celebrated her thirtieth birthday in 1954, and Mrs. Conklin had a surprise

Erma's picture was made into a postcard. She mailed one home. *Postcard courtesy Erma Bergmann.*

A three-cent stamp brought the postcard from Chicago to St. Louis in 1953. *Postcard courtesy Erma Bergamn.*

party for her in her finished basement. The basement had an outside entrance. When Mitch and Erma came through the door into the dimly lit basement, a crowd of about fifteen people shouted, "Happy Birthday!" Mrs. Conklin had prepared a fine buffet dinner for the birthday bash.

After two years of dating, Mitch told Erma, "If we get married, it would be nice if we didn't have any children." He wanted them to play golf, his favorite sport, and go fishing, her preferred pastime. He intended for them to have fun. Erma couldn't agree to not having children.

Mitch bought Erma a diamond ring but decided it wasn't pretty enough. She deserved a bigger diamond. So he hustled to the racetrack to add to his funds. Unfortunately, his horses didn't come in, and he lost his money. Erma wasn't unhappy about it. She told him he could buy her the diamond ring later on. But as it turned out, he didn't need a diamond ring. Erma decided Mitch was not ideal marriage material. She broke up with him and went home at the end of the baseball season. She thanked Mrs. Conklin for her kindness and packed her bag. Mrs. Conklin told her, "He'll go a long way before he'll find a girl like you, Erma." The two women hugged each other with tears rolling down their cheeks.

Her girlfriends told Erma, "Mitch is a playboy." His boss told her, "You went with him longer than anybody."

There's no love like a first love.

"I never forgot him. I always hoped he might call," Erma said. He did call one time when he was passing through St. Louis on business. He was already married to a beautiful blonde five years older than him. A hairdresser who owned a beauty shop, the woman had been previously married and didn't have children. She had money and presumably couldn't get pregnant. "She had everything I didn't have," Erma said. "The men I liked had something wrong with them, and the ones I could have I didn't want. I guess I'm just unlucky in love."

Love may have eluded Erma, but her success on the diamond was real. In her professional career, she pitched 1,046 innings with an earned run average of 2.56. Erma and the other players didn't realize at the time what a mark they had made in baseball history. It wasn't until years later that they realized they were pioneers on a field dominated by men.

Erma Bergmann played eight years of amateur softball and nine years of professional baseball. It had been a good run. She turned in her uniform, packed her Marty Marion glove and spikes and pointed the convertible to St. Louis. The question she asked herself was, "What does a thirty-year-old retired professional baseball player do with the rest of her life?"

9

CHANGING COURSE

Erma arrived home to a family eager to have their celebrity daughter under their roof again. She ended her baseball career with wonderful memories, close friendships and a crooked little finger. Her finger had not been broken, but she was told a fluid sac on the joint had burst. Regardless, she enrolled in a refresher typing class at Saint Louis University Adult Education School with an eye toward entering the business world.

The misfortunes of the Great Depression—long breadlines and camps of cardboard shacks called Hoovervilles—were still etched in Americans' memories. Remembering the hard times, Erma decided it was important to choose a job with security. She applied for a civil service position. People of the 1950s considered a civil service job to be safe and to provide perks such as vacation, sick leave and retirement benefits. She completed applications for city, state and federal positions and decided to take whichever one came first. The City of St. Louis won. She landed a job as a clerk in the City Assessor's Office working for John Poelker, who later became mayor of St. Louis.

Now back at home, Erma renewed some old friendships. One of her longtime St. Louis buddies was Rosemary Lyons. Rosemary and Erma had played softball together on the All-Star team in 1944. Rosemary married and ended her ball career. She and Erma lived in the same neighborhood and often enjoyed the Compton Heights Band concerts on summer nights at Francis Park. When Erma decided to officially join the Catholic Church in the year 2000, Rosemary was her sponsor. The two were friends for sixty-four years.

Erma's life seemed to be floating along on an even keel. She adjusted to being home again, she had a decent job and she enjoyed her former softball friends. The waters of her life were placid, maybe too calm. Erma thrived on challenges. She seemed to need another hurdle to jump. She needed something to pump the adrenaline through her veins like it had pulsed when she pitched in extra innings of a tied game.

One of the windows in the City Assessor's Office overlooked the St. Louis Metropolitan Police Academy across Twelfth Street, now Tucker Boulevard. Erma remembered Bertha "Billie" May Mulberg, who had been a catcher in her softball league. Billie's father's bakery sponsored the team on which she and Erma played.

As an adult, Billie became a matron in the police department. Matrons worked with juveniles, counseled wayward girls and patrolled saloons. Eventually, Billie became a commissioned policewoman.

Some years later, Billie, a heavy smoker, developed emphysema. In the last days of her life, Erma stayed with her every night. Billie said, "Of all the people I know, little did I ever think you'd turn out to be my best friend. God will take care of you."

Erma replied, "I hope maybe someday He will." From all appearances, God took good care of Erma. And she thanked Him every night for her fine parents, her good health and her exciting life.

Maybe her early association with Billie led her toward the police department. Erma also knew Marie Moyer, who was a member of the first recruitment class to accept women. Erma watched the cadets and police officers come and go and muttered to herself, "I could do that."

Welcome, new challenge. Erma was ready to climb another peak and crash into another men's arena.

Women were as rare in police departments in the 1950s as precious stones during the Depression. They were so unusual in St. Louis that the May 1951 edition of the *Police Journal* featured one of these exceptional women, Mildred Sparks, a desk sergeant in the Maplewood Police Department. The article recounted Maplewood Police officers escorting into their headquarters a man who had been celebrating too long and hard. They propped him up and asked the desk sergeant to book him. The drunk came to life quickly when he heard a pleasant, decidedly feminine voice ask his name. Turning to the police officer, the drunk muttered, "I musta had one too many—I could swear that's a woman desk sergeant." Then he passed out.

Chief Leo F. Buck had high praise for Millie Sparks. He said, "She proved that women can do a job which we thought could be handled only by a man." When asked if he planned to hire any other women, he smiled and shook his head. "No," he said. "We have no future plans. I don't think it's possible to find another Millie!"

There were more Millies around than Chief Buck imagined. One of them was named Erma.

Police Academy

This silhouette marks Erma's entrance into the world of policing. *Courtesy Erma Bergmann. Artist unknown.*

In 1915, the General Assembly of the State of Missouri provided that cities of five thousand inhabitants or more should be empowered to appoint policewomen as members of their police forces. The St. Louis Board of Police Commissioners chose to call them matrons and assigned them to duty as policewomen.

By 1919, there were fifteen matrons in St. Louis, the quota. They had no uniforms but wore nickel shields on their lapels that showed their number and "St. Louis Police Department Policewoman." They were valuable in detecting shoplifters, fortune tellers and female criminals, as well as thieves at society functions.

Sometimes, they answered advertisements for servants and worked as domestics to detect suspected criminals. One matron worked for two weeks as a waitress in a restaurant in order to uncover criminal actions that had been reported. She found that the charges were false.

In 1951, the academy graduated seven women. These female officers had the same authority as men, carried guns, wore badges and made arrests. The front-page headline of St. Louis's *Police Journal* of July 1954 screamed, "Policewomen to Be in July 26 Recruit Class."

"The Police Academy will go 'co-educational' starting with the class of forty-two men and six women trainees who will be sworn in as probationary officers," the article read. "The men represent the finalists of a pool of one hundred fourteen applicants who took stiff mental and physical examinations, followed by personal interviews before a panel of Police Board members, Chief Jeremiah O'Connell, Assistant Chief Casey and Inspector Parkes."

"The women followed the same procedure," concluded the article, almost as an afterthought.

Patrolwomen Patricia Murphy and Phoebe Blunk were the first female officers assigned to the Traffic Division in the late summer of 1954. A few years later, Phoebe and Erma were partners in special assignments. New uniforms of skirts, white blouses, long dark ties and three-cornered caps were designed for the policewomen.

Seeing herself on the cutting edge of law enforcement serving the residents of St. Louis as a female pioneer in the police department, Erma applied for admission to the academy in 1955. She was rejected, much to her disappointment and surprise. The letter stated that she was turned down because of a heart ailment. She visited her doctor, who reported that her heart was normal. Because of women's minority status in the police department in the 1950s, Erma felt the heart condition was an excuse to keep her out of the academy. She made no attempt to prove the injustice or to dispute it. She knew what she was up against. There were only about 10 women out of 1,880 police officers in the department at that time. But Erma was not programmed to fail.

She nursed her hurt and let the next couple of recruitment classes go by. She continued her clerical work in the City Assessor's Office. Then one day she was introduced to State Senator Michael Kinney. She told him about the department's refusal to admit her, and he said, "They should be glad to have a woman like you in the police department."

Buoyed by this encouragement, Erma reapplied and was admitted to the summer 1956 class of recruits. In her usual fine style, she excelled in the twelve-week training program. Her athletic prowess served her well. Her notebook—the record of her accomplishments and her notes from the academy lectures—was one of three notebooks from the sixty-four recruits to be reviewed by the police board. The three recruits were honored to represent their class by having their notebooks chosen for review. Erma was proud of this accomplishment.

On the pistol range, Erma's hand clutched a gun instead of a baseball, and her strong pitching arm was extended straight out from her chest. Her excellent vision eyed the target. Her composite score for her pistol training was 96.4 out of a possible 100 for both left and right hands, slow fire and quick fire. She was awarded a bull's-eye medal, which she could wear on her uniform after graduation. She kept the medal as a memento.

Erma also excelled in judo. Sergeant Krause, her judo instructor, selected her to demonstrate with him on the Dottye Bennett and Curt Ray television show. When they arrived at Channel 2, Sergeant Krause prompted Erma. "I'm wearing a cup," he confided. "So make it look real."

The television camera whirred. During the demonstration, the sergeant's strong arm curled around Erma's neck in a choke hold. In response, her knee came up and struck him in the groin. After the show, Krause told Erma: "You made it look real all right, Miss Bergmann. You moved the cup for me."

"I'm good at following orders, Sergeant," Erma remembered saying with a smile.

Graduation was September 5, 1956. The class consisted of two groups of recruits, the eighteenth and nineteenth classes since the academy training program was expanded to a twelve-week course in 1948. Erma and two other women were in the combined graduating class.

The sixty-four probationary patrolmen actually began police duty before they graduated. On completion of their classroom work, they were immediately assigned to parade duty and detail at the Mid-America Jubilee, a festival held on St. Louis's riverfront beginning on August 31, 1956. Erma enjoyed walking the grounds as well as seeing and hearing headliner Eddie Fisher croon "Anytime." The handsome pop singer brought teenage girls to their knees with his many hits from the 1950s. Erma began to think that police duty was pretty nice. When the jubilee closed on September 30, she and the other new patrolmen received assignments to a district.

Graduation from the academy was an important event in Erma's life. Mayor Raymond R. Tucker and Congresswoman Leonor K. Sullivan attended the recruit graduation. The *Police Journal* reported the marching demonstration of snappy drilling that pleased the dignitaries and recruits' families. A photo shows Erma Mary Bergmann shaking hands with Inspector of Police James F. Thompson, who conducted the graduation program.

Police Board president I.A. Long addressed the class:

Every complaint you investigate, every report you make out, every person you arrest—almost everything you do as you go about your daily work— becomes part of the total picture of fighting crime in our community. There are hundreds of people like you doing their daily work against crime. Step back occasionally and take a look at the big picture.

There is a frightful increase in criminal activity by young people. Today, two-thirds of all persons charged with crimes in St. Louis are sixteen years old and under.

Considering that these statistics were recorded more than seventy years ago, juvenile crime must not be a new phenomenon. Lieutenant Colonel Antoinette Filla, promoted in March 2011 to deputy chief, commander of the Bureau of Criminal Investigation and Support, was surprised by President Long's juvenile crime statistics. "Well, there may have been juvenile crime then, but drugs weren't as prevalent as they are now. And there may have been gangs, but there wasn't the violence you see now," explained Colonel Filla.

The graduation ceremony concluded with congratulatory telegrams from Lieutenant Governor James T. Blair Jr., Missouri Attorney General John Dalton and the Sisters of St. Anthony's Hospital.

KXOK Radio broadcast its congratulations and aired, "We know you will live up to the fine tradition that you inherit today."

St. Louis criminals, beware. Policewoman Erma Mary Bergmann, badge no. 100, was reporting for duty.

10

THE LADY IN BLUE

I knew more about the hoodlums in St. Louis than anybody.
I did my job and didn't say nothin'. I didn't want to wear concrete boots.
—Patrolman Erma Bergmann, Hoodlum Squad

Erma's initial reaction to her new job was amazement at the amount of crime in St. Louis. She found it depressing. During her baseball career she had traveled, even out of the country, and had met hundreds of people, but her contacts and conduct were protected by the team chaperone and by her teammates.

But now, one of only a handful of women police officers, she was thrown into a man's world of protecting the citizens of St. Louis. She served in a variety of assignments, including in the Juvenile Division, where she investigated complaints and worked with runaways. She always seized the opportunity to counsel youngsters and to try to steer them in the right direction.

"I only wrote one ticket in my twenty-five years on the force. I was riding with a sergeant, and we saw a car parked in front of a fireplug. He told me to write him a ticket."

About this time, McMahon Ford had a "Red, White and Blue Sale," and Erma bought a shiny, new blue 1965 Ford. This was the first of only two new cars she purchased in her lifetime. The other new car was a Saturn. The rest were used cars. It should have been yellow instead of blue, because it was a lemon, she remembered. The pistons did not charge correctly, so Erma took it back to the salesman. Because she had done him a favor in the past in establishing bond for his friend in jail, he had the motor replaced in her new car. Otherwise, Erma thinks she would have been stuck with a lemon.

Erma's career path crossed Lieutenant Colonel Antoinette Filla's thirty years ago, when they both worked on sex crimes. "Erma started the interviews and arrests and did the entire investigation when rape was involved," Colonel Filla remembered. "The victim almost always knew who the perpetrator was," she added.

Colonel Filla thought back to the 1970s and 1980s, when she and Erma worked together. She didn't remember Erma having any difficulty with her male counterparts. "She got along with the male officers, because she was outgoing and personable. But it's a boys' club, and they don't want to let you in. Although we do have some female sergeants and even captains, very few women get promoted. St. Louis isn't ready for high-ranking female officers," she said. "They kind of tolerate them."

Toni Filla's series of promotions defied the norm for women in the police department. In 1987, she was the first woman to be promoted to the rank of lieutenant. She became captain six years later. In 2007, she achieved the rank of major, which placed her in one of the top eleven positions in the St. Louis Metropolitan Police Department. She was named lieutenant colonel in January 2009.

Along the way, she successfully completed the highly respected FBI National Academy training program. During her career, she facilitated a networking and support group for female officers, assisting them in their career development. Colonel Filla retired in 2012 after thirty-nine years of service to the citizens of St. Louis.

"I'm a lot farther than I ever thought I would be in a man's world," the lieutenant colonel admitted the year before she hung up her badge. The difference between Erma's era and Toni Filla's is that women in Erma's police department knew they would not be promoted, so they didn't expect it or pursue it. By the time Filla had worn the blue uniform for a number of years, women were beginning to come into their own, and although she might not have expected to progress, she at least could hope. For Erma, that hope was a pipe dream.

However, she and Celeste Ruwe, her counterpart on the Rape Squad, were encouraged to go to college to advance in their career. Celeste took advantage of the department's offer and was promoted after her education was completed.

By this time, Erma's father was a patient at Jefferson Barracks Hospital, suffering from dementia. Erma called in some favors, pulled some strings and was able to have her dad admitted to the Veterans Administration Hospital. In the meantime, her mother had suffered a stroke. So Erma's hands were tied caring for her parents, and night school was impossible for her.

The smoke from Captain John Doherty's smoldering cigar curled in the air when he made the decision to pull Erma away from sex crimes and into his Hoodlum Squad to keep the files. The work was confidential, and the captain knew Erma could keep her mouth shut. She had no problem keeping the confidential information in her head and off her lips. "I didn't want to wear concrete boots," she explained, referring to the possibility of being pushed off a bridge into the Mississippi River by an infuriated hoodlum if she leaked any information about St. Louis's big-time gangsters. "I knew more about the hoodlums in St. Louis than anybody. I did my job and didn't say nothin'," she recalled.

Names like Tony Lopiparo and Tony Giordano, his assistant, rolled off her tongue like she met them yesterday. Both gangsters went to prison in 1958 for evading taxes. Lopiparo died in jail in 1960 at age forty-six.

The gangs battled one another. The Rats clashed with their Irish rivals, the Hogan gang. The Cuckoos of the near south side tried to destroy the Sicilian-immigrant Green Ones and other mob factions. The Green Ones evolved into the city's postwar "Mafia," according to Daniel Waugh, whose hobby of collecting data on St. Louis's gangland led to two books on the subject.

Erma knew all the details of the Mafia operation in St. Louis. This was an active and feared chain of gangsters fighting their opponents for territory and power. The Leisure family, "Paulie," his brother Anthony and cousins David and Ray, had fat files in Erma's office. Jimmy Michaels and his sister Sadie Faheen were part of the local Mafia. Erma knew them by her records. Michaels was murdered in September 1980, when his car exploded on Highway 55.

Erma worked for Captain Doherty, who later became a lieutenant colonel, for four years. The Hoodlum Squad was later named the Intelligence Unit, and the group continued to follow the big-time hoodlums, robbers and burglars in the city. When it came time to try them in court, Erma had the information needed to prosecute them.

While on the Hoodlum Squad, Erma also responded to special assignments. Her department was tipped off that a big-time burglar whom the police had been trying to locate for quite some time was expected to arrive at his girlfriend's house one evening. Erma was instructed to sit in the girlfriend's house and apprehend the burglar when he appeared. Other police officers were hiding around the house, ready to assist her. Erma waited nervously in

Captain John Doherty requested Erma join his department to keep the confidential records for the Hoodlum Squad. *Courtesy St. Louis Police Department Library.*

the living room. Adding to her apprehension was a bird flying from room to room. As Erma stared at the front door, waiting for it to swing open, the bird dive-bombed into the living room, lifting himself up high, then dive-bombing again.

"I was about to shoot the bird," she remembered. "He made me more nervous than I already was." The ordeal ended when the burglar did not show up, apparently tipped off that the police were waiting for him.

In another incident, Erma was detailed to a tavern about 1:00 a.m. The police thought a holdup was scheduled when the tavern closed for the night. Erma sat in the tavern, waiting for the holdup. The clock ticked. It was stressful. The tavern closed without incident. The holdup had been canceled. The burglar must have used his sixth sense and determined it was not safe to hold up the tavern and steal the money.

Erma remembers booking Glennon E. Engleman, DDS, a dentist suspected of shooting James D. Bullock, a twenty-seven-year old Union Electric Company clerk. Erma recalled Dr. Engleman as arrogant. His high-profile case was followed closely by the media. Bullock was shot three times and died near the scene in front of the Art Museum in Forest Park.

Engleman's former wife had married Bullock within a year of their divorce. Engleman was never convicted of the murder, but he was implicated in six other murders. He denied all the charges. In a surprise move, he pleaded guilty of the November 1977 shooting of Arthur and Vernita Gusewelle in their farmhouse near Edwardsville, Illinois, as well as the shooting and beating of their son Ronald Gusewelle two years later. Engleman died in March 1999 of complications from diabetes in the infirmary of the Jefferson City Correctional Center.

Erma enjoyed the perks that came with her job. She got wind of the fact that Lindburg Cadillac on Market Street near Jefferson Avenue gave police officers a discount on Cadillacs. Over a period of years, she bought five used two-door, sporty Coupe de Villes from Lindburg Cadillac. Fancy cars must have appealed to the Bergmann offspring. Erma's brother Otto drove six new convertibles in his lifetime.

Both Bergmanns had a passion for traveling, and the sister and brother sometimes vacationed together. It was in the 1970s, when Erma and Otto were deep-sea fishing off the coast of Miami, that Erma landed a thirty-seven-and-one-half-pound amberjack. It took her half an hour to haul it into the chartered fishing boat. The owner of the nearby hotel asked Erma for the fish.

Fishing was one of Erma's pleasures in life, and she fished in the Atlantic and the Pacific Oceans, the Great Lakes and any other bodies of water where the fish were biting.

She also enjoyed music and called it her second love after sports. In her early police days, she was assigned to Kiel Auditorium for the appearance of Elvis Presley. "I saw him twice, once before he went in service and a second time after he got out," Erma recalled. Both shows were sold out, according to Erma's memory. She remembered the bobbysoxers swooning and his throwing his sweaty handkerchiefs into the frenzied audience. The lucky recipients promised to never wash those handkerchiefs.

"I could have went for him, too," Erma smiled, "but there was Priscilla."

Erma joined the International Police Association and traveled with the group to Switzerland, Austria and Germany. In Germany, she was the unofficial interpreter. She spoke German fluently, as her family had spoken it at home when she was growing up. When the tour bus headed for Italy, the group laughingly threatened to put Erma off the bus, since she could no longer interpret for them.

Erma and another female officer entertained policewomen from England and Australia through the International Police Association.

The organization advertised, "The IPA offers something a travel agency cannot, because nobody knows a city or town like the police officer who lives and works there."

She enjoyed the Oktoberfest in Munich, Germany, in 1970, drinking beer and riding the Ferris wheel. Her cousin Otto invited her to return in 1972 for the Olympics. Erma accepted the invitation and returned to Munich two years later. She bought a $100 black-market ticket to the opening night of the Olympics. When it was announced that Palestinian terrorists had massacred eleven coaches and athletes, a pall fell over the city. Erma distinctly remembered how hurt and sad everyone was about the tragedy. She agreed with everyone that political differences should not intrude in sports.

Another perk for Erma was the offer to work overtime, or secondary, as the department called it, as security at Busch Stadium during Cardinal games. There were two or three policewomen in uniform who patrolled the stadium, keeping order in the stands and inspecting the ladies' restrooms. During one game, Erma caught some women stealing souvenirs from kids. Erma was in charge of the stadium operation, selecting the policewomen and rotating them to give them fair and equal turns. She earned four dollars an hour for the extra work. "If it was anywhere else but the ballpark, I wouldn't be working secondary," she told her boss.

Along the way, Erma met Mrs. Baskowitz, a friend of Police Chief James Chapman. Mr. Baskowitz had a profitable business manufacturing beer bottles for Anheuser-Busch. His wife became Erma's friend and took her to Florida for a vacation. Erma had never seen such luxury. Mrs. Baskowitz had a full-length fur coat and a butler, and she drove a Mercedes. Wired music filled Erma's bedroom. The two women had dinner by candlelight. Mrs. Baskowitz wanted Erma to replace her bourbon with scotch. She wanted her new friend to have the best.

When Erma celebrated her fiftieth birthday, Mrs. Baskowitz arranged to treat Erma and her family to dinner at the Stadium Club at the ballpark. Erma invited her mother, father and two brothers and signed the bill to be paid by her benefactor.

After Mr. Baskowitz passed away, his widow wanted Erma to move to Florida and live with her. Erma explained she couldn't leave her aging parents. Her place was in St. Louis to take care of them when they needed her help.

"All of these good things that happened to me are attributed either to sports or police work," Erma acknowledged. "During my life, I've met everybody from bag ladies to millionaires." Mrs. Baskowitz stood at the top of the heap.

When Stix, Baer & Fuller, a downtown department store, had a fur sale, Erma was assigned to patrol the department in uniform and protect the merchandise from theft. After the sale, she talked to the buyer, negotiated a discounted price and became the proud owner of a Persian lamb jacket with a mink collar. She stored the fur jacket at the Fur and Leather Centre Company in St. Louis County.

An event outside the police department catapulted Erma into the role of decision maker of the family. It was 1959 when the city announced the Kosciusko Project, a development plan to replace a sixty-seven-block area on the near south side with commercial establishments and industries. Some existing companies in the area would be able to expand operations. These companies included American Car Foundry, AnheuserBusch Inc., Monsanto Chemical Company (where Erma had been a painter), Nooter Boiler Corporation and Bemis Bros. Bag Company.

The project covered 221 acres, from Second to Seventh Streets. The purpose of the project was to bring new development into the South Broadway area, which the St. Louis Land Clearance for Redevelopment Authority called "predominantly white slum."

It was true. The neighborhood had declined during the forty years the Bergmanns rented the flat. But the development plan was about to jolt the Bergmann family like a head-on car collision. The Kosciusko Project uprooted almost six hundred families, and the wrecker's headache ball loomed over the flat on South Broadway where Erma had been born.

It was not Erma's nature to sit idly by, wringing her hands in despair. Her style was to take matters into her capable hands. She began reading the real estate section of the newspaper and found a house in the Bevo area. It was a sturdy South St. Louis home of buff brick with white stone trim around the arched front door. It was only a few years old. The living room was accented with a cove ceiling and colorful art glass windows on both sides of the fireplace. It had two bedrooms and a small hall room. There was an attic and a full basement. It was owned by a carpenter who had added some handsome finishing touches.

The house cost $24,000. The only problem was that the Bergmann family did not have $24,000. But Erma's father had inherited property in Union, Missouri, that had belonged to the Bergmann Bakery when the company provided sweets and breads for the Civilian Conservation Corps during the Depression. Erma traveled to Union and sold the property for $10,000. She

When the Bergmann family had to leave their flat on South Broadway, Erma negotiated to buy this house in the Bevo neighborhood of South St. Louis for $24,000. *Courtesy Erma Bergmann.*

admitted she knew nothing about buying or selling real estate, but she was able to come up with a $10,000 down payment for the new house. She and Otto paid the $14,000 mortgage in about ten years.

The next hurdle was convincing her father that he had to move. He decided he was not budging. Erma tried to explain to him that the whole neighborhood would soon be torn down, but he refused to go. She finally told him that the rest of the family was moving. She asked him if he loved her mother, and he replied, "Yes." Erma said, "I thought so." She left the room, and he started packing.

The house seemed like a mansion to the Bergmanns. Erma's younger brother Victor finished off an area of the basement, installed a bar and hung the German cuckoo clock behind the bar. They named the rathskeller area the "Cuckoo Bar."

Victor married, and when his wife was about to have their baby, Erma and her mother hosted a baby shower in the Cuckoo Bar. The celebration was fitting for a first grandchild-to-be. The expectant mother opened the gifts, and Erma leaned her ear against her sister-in-law's tummy and felt the baby squirming in the womb.

A couple of days later, Erma got a telephone call at the police station. Victor was at City Hospital. The doctor said both the mother and the baby might die. Erma rushed to the hospital, and her brother broke down in tears. The baby died a short time later. The family was shocked by the tragedy.

The mother lived and recovered physically. Erma disposed of the baby gifts from the recent shower, and the family prepared for Victor's wife to come home without a baby. She, however, apparently was not prepared. She did not recover emotionally and wanted a divorce. Victor moved back home.

About this time, Erma's police career took a dangerous, hairpin turn. She was about to become a sitting duck at the mercy of robbers and rapists.

11

IT'S A DECOY!

You bet I was scared. You'd have to be drunk or on something to not be scared.
—Policewoman Erma Bergmann

Erma was thirty-seven years old and had been on the police force for five years when she became part of the historic Decoy Squad, the first in the United States.

It was around 3:00 a.m. Erma was in plain clothes, instructed to pose as a prostitute as she strolled along Olive Street in Gaslight Square, a hot entertainment and art district near St. Louis's Central West End. The musicians had packed their instruments and gone home. The nightclubs, restaurants and antiques shops were closed. The usually boisterous area was quiet.

Suddenly, a voice from an alley pierced the darkness. "Hey, baby," a man yelled. Erma had a transmitter the size of a pack of cigarettes hanging from a chain around her neck. She wore a small earpiece hidden by her thick auburn hair.

Her partners in a nearby hidden police car heard the man's voice and instructed Erma to cross from the southwest corner to the northwest corner so she could be protected if her assailant attacked her. Her partner was then in position to capture him.

It was necessary that a crime be committed before an arrest could be made. The officers had to allow the criminal to complete the crime. The purpose of the Decoy Squad was to set up a situation that prompted a criminal to act. The perpetrator could be arrested for attacking a protected member of the Decoy Squad instead of a defenseless citizen. The squad sought to remove a robber or rapist from the street before he or she could harm an innocent victim.

Erma, as the decoy, was dependent on her partners' abilities to protect her. What if they couldn't get to her in time? What if the perpetrator had a weapon? She teetered on the edge of danger.

The man behind the voice appeared at the mouth of the alley. "I'm going to catch the streetcar up there," Erma told him in a hoarse voice. Fear almost locked her vocal cords. The truth was that the streetcar hadn't run on that street for a long time. Erma hoped the man in the alley didn't know that.

She started walking toward the presumed streetcar route when she passed a Salvation Army facility. A security guard stepped out from the building, and her assailant disappeared. She always felt that the security guard saved her life.

Her police partner at the time advised her, "Shoot first, then ask questions."

Erma told him later, "I can't shoot a man for saying, 'Hey, baby.' I have to live with myself."

"Were you afraid?" she was often asked.

"You bet I was scared. You'd have to be drunk or on something to not be scared."

"The Decoy Squad men are dedicated men, and their work is the most dangerous and hazardous in the Department," said the chief of detectives, Lieutenant Colonel John Doherty. He used the word *men* collectively, not with the intention of excluding women. "The main objective of the Squad is to prevent crime from happening. It's to strike fear into the potential mugger and stick-up man," Doherty said.

Erma's mind drifted back to the day in 1961 when she and Phoebe Blunk were called before the police board. The policewomen had no idea why they were summoned. H. Sam Priest, then chairman of the police board, explained to the women that the department was instituting a new program to apprehend robbers, sex offenders and criminals who prey on defenseless women. Phoebe and Erma, the only women handpicked for this special assignment, would be asked to pose as prostitutes or defenseless elderly women walking the streets in high-crime areas of St. Louis. They would work with two policemen. Radio transmitters would keep them in communication with one another. All four officers would carry pistols.

The board of police commissioners described the dangers involved and asked Phoebe and Erma if they were willing to accept the assignment. They both agreed to accept the job, which had only one guarantee: to shoot adrenaline through their veins.

"Was I supposed to say I was afraid?" Erma asked. "'They' would have said, 'why did you join the police force?'"

So Erma and Phoebe, the only women on a five-officer team, constituted a radio-equipped, undercover squad in the St. Louis Metropolitan Police Department. The specially trained group was technically called the Operative Deployment Squad. Erma took advanced training in marksmanship and judo to qualify for the team. The newspapers learned of the new unit and dubbed it the "Decoy Squad." Again, Erma found herself on the edge of danger and a pioneer in law enforcement.

A *St. Louis Globe-Democrat* headline read, "They Make Streets Unsafe for Criminals at Night." When the department became aware of an epidemic of purse-snatching from elderly women in a particular neighborhood, Erma disguised herself with a gray wig, her mother's black oxford shoes and an empty purse and assumed a feeble, awkward gait. In the black of night, she walked down the street seemingly alone, waiting for someone to grab her purse. Her partners in a nearby unmarked police car were ready, too. She only hoped they reached her in time to prevent her from being hurt and to apprehend the robber in the act of stealing her purse. When that happened, word spread quickly on the street. Robbers were leery, and residents were safer than before.

In the two months of the Decoy Squad's existence, Erma walked more than three hundred miles on streets in high-crime areas of the city. She averaged almost eight miles a night through dark alleys and streets, acting as a human clay pigeon.

"No territory is too rough for these girls," Sergeant Edward Harper told a *St. Louis Post-Dispatch* reporter. Sergeant Harper was head of the Decoy Squad and a veteran of nineteen years on the St. Louis police force. "We don't go into a territory unless it's rotten. The girls [Erma and Phoebe] are doing real 'he-man' police work. They're right in here fighting and shooting with us."

Erma's mother worried about her daughter and her dangerous line of work every time Erma left the house. Erma reminded her that she would get $30,000 if she was killed in the line of duty. Her mother could pay off the house and move to a better one, Erma reasoned. Her mother said that she didn't want to live if something happened to Erma.

June 28, 1961, was a hot, sticky St. Louis evening. The Decoy Squad was on assignment, working its normal hours of 6:00 p.m. to 2:00 a.m. Erma rode in the front seat of one of the "cover" cars. Their attention was riveted on Detective Harold Siefert, a member of the squad who on this night posed as an inebriated man. He staggered slowly down the sidewalk, weaving from side to side. Suddenly, an SOS came over the radio from Detective Siefert into the unmarked police car that carried Erma and the driver. Siefert reported that two men were following him on Franklin Avenue. The men moved close to Siefert and warned him to keep walking ahead. Then they disappeared into an alley and reappeared as he passed a vacant lot. They grabbed him and forced him into the lot.

Detective Siefert had been "jumped" six times in the ten weeks he had been a member of the Decoy Squad. He drew his revolver and identified himself as a policeman. Other members of the squad listened to Siefert on their two-way radios and hurried to help. They arrived just as the two men attempted to strong-arm and rob the detective.

One of the robbers submitted to arrest, but the other one twisted out of Detective Siefert's grasp and ran through the vacant lot. Siefert chased him and fired two shots as the robber ran through an alley to Nineteenth Street, then north to Franklin Avenue. Here he attempted to climb the fence of Franklin School.

Chief of Detectives James Shea (*right*) congratulates Erma after she shot a suspect as he scaled a fence to escape. Detective Harold Siefert (*left*), a member of the Decoy Squad, was accosted by the suspect during a Decoy Squad maneuver. St. Louis Globe-Democrat *photo, June 28, 1961, provided by Mercantile Library.*

Erma and Detective Thomas Crowe, driving the squad cover car and listening to the action on their radios, hurried to the scene. Just as they rounded a corner, they spotted a man going over the fence. Crowe ordered Erma to shoot from the car window and passenger seat where she sat. She thrust her straight arm through the open window, took aim and squeezed the trigger. A bullet from her revolver struck the man in the seat of the pants. He hung on the sharp steel pickets for a moment, then dropped limply to the ground.

"Did you hit him?" Detective Crowe asked her.

"Well if I didn't, he's sure putting on a good act," Erma replied.

"Not bad shooting when you can hit a moving target from a moving car," Sergeant Harper said later.

"It was just like on the shooting range," Erma said. "I had a mental picture of the bull's eye and aimed for that."

"It's part of the job," Erma told the *Post-Dispatch* writer, who described her as mild-mannered and soft-spoken. "I knew what the situation was. Detective Siefert had been attacked by this man. The man was trying to escape. There was nothing to do but shoot."

Erma kept the empty casing from the shot on her dresser at home.

The robber was searched and was found to be carrying a butcher knife and a large U-shaped piece of metal. He was booked on suspicion of attempted robbery and carrying a concealed weapon. An ambulance took him to City Hospital. His companion mugger rode in a police cruiser to jail. The Decoy Squad had just completed another arrest in its effective war on crime.

Erma remembered appearing in court to identify the young man she shot off the fence. Twenty-one-year-old Johnny Lee White sat in the courtroom chair, leaning on one side of his buttocks, keeping his weight off his wound.

She also vividly remembered coming home from work that June night, actually at five o'clock the next morning, exhausted and rattled from that evening's escapade. There to greet her outside her home was a *Post-Dispatch* photographer who wanted to take her picture holding her gun for an article describing the incident. She envisioned the headline in the next day's newspaper. "Policewoman Kills Juvenile" flashed through her mind.

She objected to her picture being published in the newspaper; her cover would be blown and she could easily be identified by the hoodlums. She felt that her safety would be compromised. She asked to call her supervisor before she allowed her picture to be taken.

James Chapman, chief of detectives, allowed her picture to be taken. "If you don't, I'll give him your picture from your personnel jacket."

So the picture of Erma holding her pistol across her chest appeared in the July 22, 1961 edition of the *St. Louis Post-Dispatch* as a teaser for the two-page feature story that appeared the next day. The headline read, "Policewomen as Decoys," followed by the tagline, "Two Bold St. Louis Officers Walk Every Night Seeking to Deter Crime."

Erma was horrified that the department had so little regard for her life and valued the publicity of their success more than her safety. The next night while walking the street on duty, she heard a voice pierce the darkness, "There goes that [expletive] policewoman." Voices erupted from the shadows, cursing her. The thought of it sent shivers up Erma's spine. Fifty years later, she still harbored a deep resentment about the department's unwillingness to protect her.

Joe Burgoon joined the police department in 1960 and retired in 2004 as a homicide detective. In retirement, he works part-time as a cold-case investigator for the St. Louis County Police. He makes the news from time to time, digging up old evidence on unsolved crimes and presenting it for examination by forensic scientists. He calls these new scientists "the real heroes." He has solved about forty cold crimes, including sexual assaults and homicides.

Sergeant Burgoon remembered Erma's shooting the suspect while he climbed a fence. "She had a short-barreled snub-nose pistol. She was a great shot. She was also very nice, laid back. She was a very classy lady."

"At one time, Erma and I worked out of the same office. We were young guys, but some of those women could knock the daylights out of you. They could take care of themselves," the career policeman remarked. "She hasn't changed at all, except for her hair [which is now white]. She took care of herself."

Three nights after the shooting incident, twenty-three shots were fired in a running gun battle between two attackers and members of the Decoy Squad. Detective Siefert was again attacked and robbed near Ninth and Cole Streets in downtown St. Louis. He had stopped momentarily at a telephone booth, unaware that two men had crept up behind him. Taken by surprise, he was unable to defend himself. The men beat him, ripped his revolver and wallet from his trousers pocket, snatched his wristwatch from his arm and knocked him to the ground.

Although badly beaten, Siefert managed to turn on his miniature radio and call the other members of the Decoy Squad for help. Detective Crowe saw one of the suspects come out of an alley and run north on Ninth Street. He stopped his car, pursued the man and grabbed him by the arm. Pulling free, the suspect drew a revolver from his pocket and shot Crowe at point-blank range. The bullet shattered the detective's kneecap. Crowe fired a return shot before collapsing on the sidewalk.

Erma and Phoebe rushed to help the wounded detective while the other members of the team called for reinforcements and chased the man to an apartment building in the Cochran housing project. Police, including members of the canine squad, searched the building and found the former convict huddled on a second-floor landing. Detective Siefert's revolver and wristwatch were still in his possession.

Sergeant Harper credits the Decoy Squad with more than two hundred arrests in its first seven months of crime fighting. Police Chief Curtis Brostron rated it "one of the most effective crime control techniques the Board of Police Commissioners initiated in the department last year."

However, the crew was disappointed in the fact that purse snatchers or rapists were few and far between in accosting Erma and Phoebe. "All the girls have attracted are mashers, so far," Sergeant Harper said one month into the new program. "We know from the way the auto-Romeos keep flocking around that the girls are not suspected of being policewomen," he said in a newspaper interview. Erma was an attractive brunette walking alone on a dark street and a temptation to men looking for a romantic rendezvous. She ignored their advances. Much to her stalkers' surprise, one of her partners seconds later startled the would-be Don Juans, asking who they were and why they were trying to pick up women on the street. Most of them were married men out on the prowl, Erma remembered.

Erma was anxious for more action and tired of hearing, "Hi babe, how about goin' for a ride?"

"I'd like to get my hands on someone who likes to rob old women," she said at the time, smoothing her housedress and adjusting her gray wig.

One of her decoy squad companions said, "Boy! I want to be around and see what happens to the punk who grabs Erma. She's the best judo expert we have in the department."

One June night in 1961, Erma strolled through a rooming house neighborhood. A voice from her cover car crackled from the closed-channel radio.

"Heads up, Erma. Someone has slipped behind you."

Back came a calm, "OK," through Erma's pocket transmitter.

The cover car moved slowly down the street until Erma and the man following her were in full view.

"He's about ten feet behind you, Erma."

Her short whistle came over the radio in reply, letting the occupants of the car know she had received the message.

The alert ended when the man turned down another street at an intersection. Erma resumed her walk.

A spotlight shone on the Decoy Squad's success, and it became the center of attention across the country. It also expanded from five to twenty-five members in January 1962, seven months after its birth. By this time, Erma and Phoebe had moved on to other assignments. Erma packed her decoy costumes away and put on her navy skirt; a crisp, white, starched shirt; a long dark tie; and a cap. When the department allowed the women to wear slacks, Erma continued to wear her skirt. "Men used to say I had pretty legs," she said.

She always carried a black leather shoulder bag that she bought for $100 when she was a police officer. It was heavy with handcuffs and a pistol. Like Erma, the purse didn't show its age. Today, the bag and its contents weigh about five pounds. She was proud of her uniform and of the work she was doing for the citizens of St. Louis.

Erma returned to duty in the Juvenile Division, although the Decoy Squad borrowed her from time to time to work in a St. Louis neighborhood where a number of attempted rapes had been reported.

The late *Globe-Democrat* staff writer Ted Schafers applauded the work of the St. Louis police Decoy Squad, referring to them as "the group of men and women who risk their lives nightly by posing as sitting ducks for criminals."

In April 1962, the local Associated Press bureau sent a story on its national wire about the St. Louis Police Decoy Squad. Criminal justice history was made when St. Louis inaugurated the decoy method of attracting and apprehending criminals. Pulp detective magazines gloried in the true stories of the city's Decoy Squad, a first in criminal justice history.

Erma received a letter from one of the readers of *True Police Detective Magazine* in October 1961. The reader, from Kenosha, Wisconsin, wrote:

> *I have been reading these detective magazines since 1947, when I was still in high school. I found the story about your work with the Decoy Squad very interesting. But your work is very dangerous. Congratulations, Miss Bergmann, for shooting that thief and causing his arrest. That stood out as the most heroic act I have ever heard of. It takes nerves of steel to do what you and Mrs. Blunk are doing on the Decoy Squad.*

Miss Bergmann, I am enclosing a St. Christopher medal for you. I would like for you to wear it. I had the medal blessed for you. It does not matter if you are a Catholic or not. You can still wear it.
Keep up the fine work you are doing. Be careful, and good luck.

"The Squad's success has led a dozen other police departments to inquire or study the operation," the AP story said. St. Louis's Decoy Squad became a national model.

"One goal of the squad is to create fear in the mind of the robber or attacker that his potential victim may be a policeman or policewoman," Chief of Detectives James Shea said.

If there was any prejudice in the police department against female cops, Erma seemed unaware of it. Her male coworkers admired her outstanding record in the St. Louis Metropolitan Police Academy and her bravery on the Decoy Squad. She regaled them with stories about her life as a baseball player. The men couldn't get enough of her narratives. They liked her straightforward, no-nonsense method of communicating. They enjoyed her sense of humor and her love of life and people.

But not all of the female employees in the police department agreed with Erma. Sandy Atherton worked with female prisoners from 1976 to 1983, and her path crossed Erma's in Prisoner Processing. Her path also crossed Erma's in 2011 over a stack of pancakes at the International House of Pancakes, formerly on Chippewa Avenue in South St. Louis. Sandy sat in an adjoining booth, and when she overheard Erma's conversation, she recognized her voice. She was delighted to talk to Erma, her former coworker whom she hadn't seen in many years. The two law enforcement women reminisced about their careers.

Sandy remembered, "It was like working in a world of Archie Bunkers," referring to the bigot who was prejudiced against everyone in the popular television show *All in the Family*. "Men would ask me, 'Why aren't you home washing windows?'"

"Because I have bills to pay," she replied. Sandy Atherton has worked in law enforcement for forty years. She earned an associate degree in criminal justice when she was in her fifties. At age sixty-six, she worked in Sheriff James Murphy's office.

Despite prejudice against women, Erma had her police admirers. One was Manuel Delgado. Manny opened A Drinking Establishment in South St. Louis about 1993 after he retired as a thirty-year police officer. The tavern's name, Area IV, was emblazoned in gold letters on the fading maroon awning that covered the wide front window.

"At one time the city was divided into three police districts. My bar became the fourth," the owner joked. Manny's hair on the back of his head is tied in a ponytail, maybe to compensate for his bald pate. It was 10:00 a.m., and the bar smelled of stale cigarette smoke and beer.

Manny was born in Laredo, Texas, where his uncle was a policeman. His father worked for General Motors and was transferred to St. Louis in 1951. Manny was a U.S. Marine from 1955 to 1958 stationed in the desert in Twentynine Palms, California. He started as a uniformed police officer in 1961 in the Seventh District at Union and Page Avenues.

"The police station was modeled after Monticello, with big pillars and a balcony on the second floor. It was a three-story building that housed about 150 policemen. It also housed the original mounted police in a small stable in the back," Manny remembered.

In 1974, Manny was promoted to sergeant and transferred to headquarters, where Erma was assigned to Prisoner Processing for the last few years of her police career. Her glory days on the force had come to an end. No more Rape, Decoy or Hoodlum Squads. No more excitement. "Assignments were doled out according to who you knew. These were city jobs and there was a lot of politics. I served my sentence. I did the hard work just like I did the easy jobs." A mundane desk job ended her police career.

"Erma was a character, very individualistic," Manny grinned. "I liked her. Her ball playing got her acquainted with the male police officers. She seemed rough, but she was as gentle as a lamb. She was very likable, a nice person."

This photo was taken by the St. Louis Metropolitan Police Department. *Courtesy Erma Bergmann.*

"I appreciated the policewomen. They could do the jobs that most men weren't trained to do. They usually started in the Juvenile Division. They were adept with women and children," said the widower with three grown children. "I lost track of how many grandchildren I have. I think I have nine and three or four great-grandchildren. When we have a family get-together, I ask them to wear name tags so I know who they belong to."

Manny's only complaint about women on the force was the fact that they changed the actuarial tables for figuring pensions. According to Manny, "The actuaries didn't factor in women's longevity, and men might receive less pension."

In Prisoner Processing, where Manny and Erma worked together, Erma booked prisoners, relieving them of the worldly possessions they carried in their purses and pockets and escorting them into a cell. The worldly possessions of old women hauled in for vagrancy or protective custody often consisted of the end of a comb with broken teeth and a piece of dried bread. When Erma reached into their pockets, the fabric would often be wet from urine. The police brought the women in at about 9.00 p.m. so they wouldn't sleep on the street or in a doorway. If there weren't enough cells, or if the police didn't want them to bunk with undesirables, the women would lie on the concrete floor. But at least they were safe.

Joe Fitzpatrick brought a female prisoner in on New Year's Eve night. After booking the prisoner, Erma abruptly stood up from her desk, planted a kiss on Joe's round Irish cheek and said, "Happy New Year."

Patrolman Dennis "Bull" Ward walked a beat and worked with Erma in Prisoner Processing. "She was a classic. You never got on Erma's bad side. She would straighten you out. And she would remember it."

Bull Ward retired from the force in 1995 and took a job with the Police Funeral Association. Erma paid $52 a year into the police funeral fund. When she died, the fund paid $4,000 directly to Kutis Funeral Home for her funeral expenses.

As the only girl in her family, Erma was the unofficial caretaker. "I took care of both my parents and my brother Victor. I went with him three times to Mayo Clinic where he was treated for colon problems," Erma recalled. Her understanding of his illness is that his enlarged colon leaked germs that penetrated his system and killed him.

"My dad died in 1972 of infirmities of old age at age eighty-six. I pulled some strings and got him into the VA Hospital in Jefferson Barracks." She visited him often on her days off from the police department, even when he couldn't remember if she worked or not.

Two years later, Erma received a call at her desk telling her about her mother's stroke. Erma rushed to the hospital. Her mother later succumbed to the stroke.

It was 1977, and Erma was still working on the police force when she learned through her old softball friend Rosemary Lyons about Anna Nesselhauf, who planned to move to Europe to join her sister and wanted to sell her unmarked crypt in Sunset Memorial Cemetery and Mausoleum. Erma bought her crypt in Building no. 6 for $500. Today, the same crypt would cost about $4,000. Erma had a knack for bargains. She had her name and birth date inscribed on the marble crypt and purchased a brass flower urn with her name encircling it.

Back in Prisoner Processing, Erma remembered a striptease artist from the DeBaliviere Strip who was arrested for prostitution. The policeman who brought her in ordered her to remove her costume and replace it with a hospital gown. She boldly refused and marched into her cell naked.

"These women spoke another language," Erma said. "I refused to use their language. It wasn't easy being a lady booking prisoners. They called me the worst names they could think of, and they knew some. I often told the women prisoners, 'How would you like to act like a lady for five minutes?'"

They also kept Erma busy asking for things—cigarettes, toilet paper, matches. She always carried a couple of extra packages of cigarettes to keep the women quiet.

Erma was a good listener. She was attentive to what the prisoners said before booking them. She didn't handle her job with authority or power. Erma's former ball-playing friends thought she was too easygoing, and they wondered how she made it as a policewoman. Her theory was that you get more done with honey than with vinegar.

Erma seemed able to encourage the women to open up to her. A sergeant thought a woman lied about being raped. Erma took her upstairs for a lie-detector test. On the way, the woman admitted that she had lied and that taking a lie-detector test was unnecessary. The prisoner then faced a less serious charge, making a false police report, a misdemeanor, instead of lying about being raped, which was a felony.

Erma remembered a prisoner who screamed all night. Another inmate threatened to spit on her and hit her. All of a sudden, the inmate fell. Erma put her foot on her leg so she could not get up. That was the end of that. Erma never knew what made her fall, but all of a sudden she was on the floor.

When a Romani was released, she told Erma, "You're a nice lady." Then she put her hands on Erma's back.

"Get your hands off me," Erma stiffened and commanded, prepared to knock the Romani to the floor if necessary. The woman removed her hands and left quietly. Other police officers told Erma: "You don't know your strength. I asked you to open the door, not hand me the door," they joked.

Erma sometimes walked into a police headquarters meeting room that reeked of cigarette smoke, exhaling her own billows into the haze. Erma had quit smoking for five years, then went back to puffing for seven years. She finally quit smoking in 1980, never again to press her lips around a cigarette.

On occasion, she would hear men talking disrespectfully about women. She merely seized the opportunity to tell them, "Remember, men. Your mother was a woman."

"That shut 'em up," Erma recalled with a smile spreading across her wrinkled face.

There were some conditions in the police department that made Erma grit her teeth, but she learned to accept them. One especially difficult part of her latter assignment was changing shifts every three weeks. She worked around the clock, 3:00 a.m. to 11:00 a.m., 11:00 a.m. to 7:00 p.m. and 7:00 p.m. to 3:00 a.m. "I read somewhere that switching shifts like that takes five years off your life," said the former police officer who turned eighty-nine years old in 2013 with a small celebration at River City Casino. Sleep experts tend to agree with Erma. Rotating schedules makes it very difficult for the brain to know when to be awake and when to be asleep, according to Raman Malhotra, co-director of the Sleep Disorders Center at St. Louis University.

"My mother had trouble keeping track of when I was supposed to get up," Erma remembered.

Another bone of contention was the fact that promotion of a female officer was out of the question in her day. Members of the police department promised her promotions, but her mentors died or retired before they could arrange her advancements. "My aces were in the cemetery. Promises, promises, that's what I got," Erma recalled.

There was discussion at one time about adding the rank of corporal and elevating Erma to that rank. But the rank was not put in place, and being promoted to sergeant was not in the realm of male thinking at that time. So, even though Erma performed her duties in exemplary fashion, she ended her twenty-five-year career as a patrolman, the same title conferred on her when she graduated from the academy.

In the 1970s, women began to climb out of obscurity and find their places in better-paying positions. There were more women on the police force than there had been when Erma entered the academy.

A cause for celebration among female athletes was Title IX, a law passed in 1972 that mandates gender equity for boys and girls in every educational program that receives federal funding, including athletics. President Richard Nixon signed the bill into law, eliminating sex discrimination in college sports and educational opportunities.

Celebrations were held on college campuses across the country for the fortieth anniversary of Title IX in 2012. Billie Jean King, winner of twenty

Wimbledon tennis championships, called Title IX "a grand slam for women." She pointed out that the number of women in college athletics jumped from 32,000 to more than 166,000 between 1972 and 2007. "Title IX was one of the most important pieces of legislation of the twentieth century," the retired tennis champion told the American Association of Retired Persons (AARP).

Leah O'Brien-Amico, three-time gold medalist for USA softball, spoke at Marshall University in San Diego for its fortieth-anniversary celebration of Title IX. "The efforts and passion for sport displayed by AAGPBL players paved the way for the passage of such a law."

Time has proven Title IX's worth. For the first time in history, there were more women than men participating in the 2012 Summer Olympics, held in London. Erma always bemoaned the fact that volleyball was the only sport offered to girls during the four years she spent at McKinley High School. Title IX corrected that deficiency.

Even though it had been years since Erma stepped off the baseball field, she still had contacts in the Cardinals organization. She celebrated her fiftieth birthday with a surprise party for six guests in the Cardinals Stadium Club. She invited her mother, her dad, her two brothers and her brother's wife. They enjoyed dinner and the Cardinals game from some of the best seats in the stadium. The Cardinals picked up the check.

Erma retired in 1981 at age fifty-six, an unusually young age. "I wasn't money hungry. I had served twenty-five years. I was single and I didn't want to work all my life. I decided I wanted to enjoy life."

About the time she retired, love bloomed again in Erma's life. It happened over a steakburger and a cup of coffee at Steak 'n Shake, one of her favorite restaurants. As a matter of fact, she had been a customer at the Hampton and Gravois location for more than sixty years, beginning when it opened in 1950. Like a rock star, she was welcomed by name when she walked through the door.

Billy Donaldson, who waited on Erma for the eight years he worked at the location, said: "Erma is somebody, but doesn't act like it. Usually people who aren't anything act like they are somebody. You don't get to meet people like Erma very often."

Rebecca Huffman, manager of the Steak 'n Shake, told Erma: "You're a legend. It's a pleasure to know someone who had a part in history."

Even a customer who played softball in his younger years got wind of Erma's baseball career and paid her bill one evening.

The best part of these friendly surroundings was chatting with Ed, another frequent customer of the eatery. Ed worked in the parts department of

Hussmann Refrigeration Company. He had played second base on a minor league team, meeting Erma's athletic criterion for a suitor.

Ed and Erma enjoyed the same things, especially betting on the horses at the racetrack. They traveled to Louisville for the 109th Kentucky Derby in the 1980s, staying in separate hotel rooms. Erma cooked dinner for Ed most nights at home. Everything was made from scratch—no frozen dinners in Erma's menu.

Ed told her, "If it hadn't been for you, I wouldn't have lived this long." He was convinced she extended his life with her good cooking. The twosome talked about getting married, but Ed lived in a house with his sister, and Erma owned a house with her brother. Neither one wanted to move. By this time in their lives, there didn't seem to be any compelling reason to marry. But they enjoyed each other's company for thirteen years until his death. Ed told her, "They broke the mold after they made you, Erma."

The police department had similar feelings for her. Police captain Bob Boaz, who retired in 1990 after almost forty years on the force, summed up Erma's police career. "Everybody knew Erma, and everybody liked her. Erma was always a lady. She was a very fine lady and a good police officer," he said.

It was well into the twenty-first century when I bumped into two lady cops who stopped in Rue Lafayette, a coffee shop and boutique across from Lafayette Park in South St. Louis, for a cup of coffee.

Over our cups of coffee, Erma became the topic of conversation. One of the policewomen said: "We're very grateful to her. She paved the way for the rest of us."

During the twenty-five years Erma spent on the police force, her baseball career was almost forgotten by everyone except her family. She and the other female players went their own ways and disappeared into the annals of sports history. That was about to change with the production of a movie that has become a favorite sports story the world over.

12

A LEAGUE OF THEIR OWN

There's no crying in baseball.
—*Tom Hanks*

Erma packed her police-issue service revolver in her purse and stowed her purchased pistol in the nightstand next to her bed. With her second career behind her, what would Erma do for excitement? It turns out that there was no need for worry. Erma was always able to make her life interesting.

Many years ago, when her nephews and niece were youngsters, Erma bought a small travel trailer. When the kids asked for a larger trailer, Erma bought one. Aunt Erma was always a pushover. Through the years, she showered Victor's children with bicycles, cars and vacations.

If strong-willed Erma has an Achilles' heel, it's her older nephew, Victor. He's named for his father, who died in 2000. Young Victor is now about forty years old. He was the most attentive to Erma and was always kind to her brother Otto during his life. In appreciation, Aunt Erma generously gave nephew Victor whatever he requested, including trips for him and his girlfriend to Hawaii, Florida and Branson.

"What's the difference? He's going to get it when I die," Erma reasoned. After Otto's death on Thanksgiving Day 2010, Victor moved into Erma's rathskeller, which his father had constructed many years before. In exchange for free rent, he was the resident repairman.

In earlier years, Otto had paired with Pat, a singer at a piano bar. The two traveled extensively until Pat had a heart attack. She came to live with Otto and Erma while she recuperated. Ten years later, Pat was hale and hearty and still there. Erma resented the intrusion, especially the fact that Otto never discussed it with her.

Nevertheless, when Pat had the stroke that eventually ended her life, Erma rode with her to the hospital in the ambulance. Pat died in 2000, and her picture was prominently displayed in Erma's living room near the fireplace.

After Pat's death, Otto seemed to have a slight stroke that affected his vision. He was no longer able to drive. Erma became his chauffeur.

In the meantime, young Victor earned his GED at Erma's insistence and eventually got a job with Enterprise Leasing Company, working in one of its garages. He had two days off in the middle of the week, and he spent one of those days with Otto at the *Casino Queen* gambling boat, giving Erma a break from her driving duties. Sometimes, Erma, who liked to gamble, went with them.

When her younger nephew, Johnny, needed a $600 clutch for his car, he came to Erma. Erma, who liked to make deals, agreed to pay for his clutch if he got his GED. Some weeks later, Johnny was proud to let her know he kept his part of the bargain.

In the late 1970s, she bought a timeshare in the Hill Country Resort at Canyon Lake near Austin, Texas. The previous owner had defaulted on the payment of $10,000, so Erma picked it up for a discounted $8,000. It was hard to resist a bargain, although she had never been to the Hill Country Resort.

In the 1990s, Erma bought another timeshare, from Silver Leaf Resorts, with locations at Timber Creek near DeSoto, Missouri, and another in Branson, Missouri. She enjoyed entertaining Otto, her single brother with whom she lived; Victor, her married brother; and his three children at these resorts. She thoroughly enjoyed the shows in Branson.

Erma's two-bedroom unit on the second floor at Timber Creek was spacious. She considered herself in the lap of luxury when she stepped into the Jacuzzi connected to her bedroom, and she enjoyed the fresh air when she and Otto sat on the front and back porches.

Erma bought a trolling motor and was almost giddy sitting in the canoe gliding across the forty-acre lake with a fishing pole in her hand. She took her German ten-speed bicycle to Timber Creek, and she and her nephews pedaled around the grounds.

Her next adventure was a shiny new 125 Harley-Davidson motorcycle. She was sixty-five years old, when many people retire and sink into a rocker. But Erma was throwing her shapely leg over the leather saddle seat, starting the motor and roaring down the street. Her broad smile mirrored her pleasure.

The Harley-Davidson ad in *Science and Mechanics* magazine of October 1951 proclaimed: "This peppy 2-wheeler gives you quick, dependable transportation at lowest cost…90 miles and more per gallon, no parking problems. Easy to ride with 3-speed transmission, 2-wheel brakes, road cushioning Tele-Glide Fork, easy chair saddle, auto type lighting."

This "peppy" vehicle matched Erma's zest for life. She and her nephew Victor rode it until Victor had a slight accident one day. Erma then put on the brakes and decided it wasn't safe to ride it in the city. She sold it back to the dealer after owning it for less than a year.

The Birth of the Players Association

In the early 1960s, about ten years after the league folded, Arnold Bauer, an usher, statistician and number one fan of the South Bend Blue Sox, and ex–business manager Ed Des Lauriers decided to attempt to locate and survey the former AAGPBL players. Mr. and Mrs. Bauer housed four Blue Sox players each year of the league's existence and probably wondered what happened to them.

The two men mailed more than 400 letters and received 148 responses, according to the AAGPBL history. The respondents reported playing softball, basketball, volleyball, field hockey, lacrosse, bowling, tennis, golf and badminton. Some of the ex-players were swimming, skating, water skiing, hunting, fishing, skiing and curling.

As they approached middle age, these women were also working or raising families, or both. Some coached, umpired or competed in sports. The common thread that connected them was total agreement that the years spent in the league were some of the best of their lives. They also agreed that they had formed lasting friendships that needed to be renewed from time to time.

The first players' reunion was held some twenty years later, in 1982 in Chicago. Erma was delighted to renew old friendships at this reunion that celebrated the league's fortieth anniversary. This first reunion sparked the formal creation of the All-American Girls Professional Baseball League Players Association. Articles of Incorporation were filed with the state of Michigan on September 9, 1987. The first business meeting was held in Fort Wayne, Indiana, with forty-five members in attendance.

A subsequent reunion celebrated the fiftieth anniversary of the founding of the league in South Bend, Indiana, home of the league's archives in the

Center for History. Erma also traveled to Palm Springs, California, for the 1995 reunion. Now they're annual events.

This resurgence of interest in the league also sparked an interest in recording the league's activities and its place in history for future generations. Helen Callaghan St. Aubin of Vancouver, Canada, played on the Minneapolis Millerettes alongside her sister Margaret. Helen was a star batter and base stealer. In 1945, at five feet, one inch and 115 pounds, she paced the league in doubles and tied for the lead in home runs. One of her sons, Casey Candaele, played for nine seasons in the major leagues. While Casey swung a bat that was thirty-three inches long and weighed thirty-two ounces, his mother's bat was thirty-six inches long and weighed thirty-six ounces.

Another of Helen Callaghan's sons, Kelly Candaele, along with Kim Wilson, produced a 1988 documentary entitled *A League of Their Own*. The twenty-seven-minute film featured the history of the league and interviews with former players.

Penny Marshall, actress, comedy writer and movie director and producer, fell in love with the documentary when a copy landed on her desk at 20th Century Fox. She thought it should be a feature film. The timing was perfect. Penny's movie *Big* had just scaled the box office milestone of $100 million. *Big* was the first movie directed by a woman to gross more than $100 million at the U.S. box office.

Television viewers felt like they knew Marshall from her starring role in the classic sitcom *Laverne & Shirley*. Sony Pictures lured her away from 20th Century Fox with the bait, "If you come with us, we'll even let you do that girls movie."

Penny Marshall's baseball film project was off and running. Many of the former players were interviewed. Marshall asked Erma if playing ball had any effect on her later life. Erma replied, "It certainly did, Penny. I learned how to get along with people and how to stand on my own two feet. You can't holler 'Momma' every time you need something."

"My uncle, the Marianist brother, said going away to play ball improved my personality 100 percent. Playing ball brought me out. My uncle was an English major and corrected my English from time to time."

Penny Marshall asked Lowell Ganz and his writing partner Babaloo Mandel to create the script for the movie. They were on a hot streak and had recently turned in the script for Steve Martin's hit *Parenthood*. The writing team agreed with Marshall that the baseball documentary had potential as a feature film.

Casting was difficult, because actresses aren't always athletes. And both skills were required. Lori Petty, scrappy, athletic and confident, fit the bill. Tom Hanks asked for the role of manager of the Rockford Peaches. Marshall's challenge was to pare down his good looks, so she told him to get fat. He ate his way through the filming in Chicago and Indiana, according to Marshall's memoir.

Marshall approached Madonna to see if she could play ball. Madonna came to New York and worked out for three hours with the coaches at St. John's University. She passed their test. They decided she was trainable, so she got the part. Several former players traveled to Skokie, Illinois, to teach actresses Geena Davis, Madonna and Rosie O'Donnell how to bat, throw and catch. Davis was a natural athlete. The main roles of the movie were cast.

Shooting began while the actresses had daily batting practice and worked on fielding their positions. This movie was going to be athletic and authentic.

The first part of the movie was shot on a farm outside Evansville, Indiana. Erma, her younger brother Victor and his two sons, Victor and Johnny, drove to Evansville to watch the filming. They pulled up near the farm and were stopped by barricades. Erma walked up to the state trooper at the barricade, flashed her winning smile and told him she was one of the ballplayers the movie was about and that she had been a policewoman in the St. Louis Metropolitan Police Department. The trooper simply said, "Go wherever you want. I don't even see you."

The Bergmanns peeked into the barn and saw the cows that the two future ballplayers would milk during the filming.

Penny Marshall describes in her memoir how, during the shoot, when the scout is giving his pitch to the would-be players, one of the cows fell over and began to give birth. The actor didn't even notice and continued his lines. The hubbub required a reshoot. The farmer named the calf "Penny."

The end of the movie was filmed at the Baseball Hall of Fame in Cooperstown, New York. The players were invited to appear in the movie, walking into the Hall of Fame to view their exhibit. Erma and her friend Audrey already had bought plane tickets to Florida for a players' reunion and declined the opportunity to fly to New York to be part of the movie.

The year 2012 marked the twentieth anniversary of *A League of Their Own*. The City of Evansville invited the former All-American Girls Professional Baseball League players to travel to the city as honored guests at a special showing of the movie. Erma decided she wanted to return to Evansville for the festivities celebrating the film's anniversary. So she, a friend who was a photographer and I, her biographer, hopped in the car and headed to the farm where Erma had witnessed the filming twenty years earlier.

Former players Eileen "Ginger" Gascon from Chicago and Dolly Konwinski and her husband Bob from Grand Rapids, Michigan, also made the trip. Ginger appeared in the movie's climax, walking into Cooperstown's Hall of Fame with other players. "Each player was paid $402 for their week's work," Ginger reported.

Finding the farm was something of a challenge for Erma and her traveling companions. Local people knew vaguely where it was, but not exactly. We were advised to stop at Weinzapfel's Tavern and General Store on the highway for directions. A sign in the tavern announced the Thursday special: one dollar for a twelve-ounce draft beer. Since the day was Thursday, we decided to return after we found the farm.

We were told that the farm is on St. Phillips Road, a drive next to St. Phillips Catholic Church and Cemetery. Venturing up the hill, we came upon a barn and a ten-room white frame farmhouse. Wilma Schenk emerged from the house, wondering who was trespassing on her property. When she learned our mission, the eighty-two-year-old mistress of the house graciously welcomed us. She had married into the Schenk family and raised four children in five rooms on the second floor of the family farmhouse. Her son played baseball on the field down from the barn where part of the movie was filmed. The original barn where Lori Petty and Geena Davis milked the cows has been torn down. But its replacement stands, and the ball field was still in view down the hill.

We left the farm and returned to Weinzapfel's Tavern. Erma held court in the crowded, friendly establishment, one elbow propped on the bar, the other hand wrapped around a cold draft beer. She cheerfully distributed signed baseball cards, obviously one of the most famous customers to sip the one-dollar draft beer at Weinzapfel's in the past twenty years.

A local lady in the tavern told Erma she had been hired as an extra for the movie. Had she been used, she would have sat in the stadium's stands in costume. Although her movie career never materialized, she was still proud of waiting in the wings.

Some of the fans in the stands during the filming were cardboard figures, we were told.

We were guests of the Evansville Convention and Visitors Bureau, which reserved rooms for us at the Le Merigot Hotel on the Ohio River across from the casino. The casino was a magnet that lured Erma to its slot machines during her free time.

This is Weinzapfel's Tavern in Evansville, Indiana, near where the movie *A League of Their Own* was filmed. Erma met a woman who was hired as an extra for the movie. *Courtesy Gene Donaldson.*

The highlight of the trip was Friday night's open-air viewing of the movie on a huge screen set up on the pitcher's mound of Bosse Field, where some of the movie was filmed. Bosse Field, home of the minor league Evansville Otters, is the third-oldest ballpark in the country. It was preceded by Fenway Park in Boston, which opened in April 1912, then by Chicago's Wrigley Field (1914). Opening Day at Bosse Field was June 17, 1915. A box seat that day cost 75 cents, the grandstand was 50 cents and a seat on the bleachers was 25 cents. When *A League of Their Own* was filmed there, the roof was added by the film company.

Erma, Ginger and Dolly sat at a table at the entrance to the stadium, signing posters and greeting fans. Ushers were dressed in nostalgic short skirts, similar to the uniforms Erma and the other players wore in the 1940s.

The league players stepped out on the field prior to the showing of the film. The crowd cheered as the ladies waved to their fans. The fans paid five dollars for general admission and eight dollars for box seats to meet the players and witness the event.

The *Evansville Courier and Press* interviewed Erma for the article "Diamond Girls—Veteran Baseball Players Turn Out for 'League' screening." An interview was also filmed at the ballpark by WFIE Channel 14.

It was a great trip down memory lane for Erma, complete with kudos for her accomplishments. Penny Marshall, who directed the film, shared the

This television interview was filmed at historic Bosse Field, where part of the movie was filmed. Bosse Field opened in 1915 and is now home to the Evansville Otters. *Courtesy Gene Donaldson.*

kudos when she became an honorary member of the players' association at the reunion in San Diego in 2012. "If it had not been for you, Penny, no one would ever have known that we existed," the league players said in their official bimonthly publication, *Touching Bases.*

The Center for History in South Bend, Indiana, is home to the largest collection of artifacts of the All-American Girls Professional Baseball League. The center celebrated the film's twentieth anniversary with a special display for visitors to the museum.

A League of Their Own made more than $100 million, and it's still shown on television regularly. In 2013, the Library of Congress selected the film for inclusion in the National Film Registry as "culturally, historically or aesthetically significant." The registry was established in 1989 to preserve U.S. film heritage for future generations, and the twenty-five movies selected that year brought the total in the registry to six hundred. The films must be at least ten years old.

"These films are works of enduring importance to American culture," Librarian of Congress James M. Billington said. "They reflect who we are as a people and as a nation."

13

THE GLORY DAYS

Dear Ms. Erma Bergmann,

How do you do? I have been a biggest fan of you since I met you on baseball materials. I bet baseball is the most beautiful game in the world. I respect your play in the ballpark and your human nature. I feel encouraged by you and the wonderful feats of the All American Girls Professional Baseball League. I have been studying all of baseball history in your great country. So I'm honored to make contact with you via air mail this time.

Please may I have your autograph on my card?

Sincerely yours,

For Love of the Game

Kohei Nirengi

Japan

Erma's mailman delivered fan mail from all corners of the world almost every day. Answered letters are piled high in her closet. "It's a job to keep up with the mail and sign the things people send," she said. "But I answer every letter." Erma and her teammates double as goodwill ambassadors for our country.

Helen Varga of Imperial Beach, California, ended her handwritten note by writing, "You ladies occupy a very special place in baseball history."

A recent letter from Singapore and a box of materials to sign and return required Erma to hop in her 1999 Dodge Sport van with the speedometer reading 120,000 miles and drive to the post office to send the box overseas.

As *A League of Their Own* played on screens across the United States and around the world, baseball fans began to wonder about the actual players. Who are these women who dared to infringe on the man's world of baseball?

Erma began to receive requests for speaking engagements. Her life revolved around *A League of Their Own*. Even her nephew Victor, who had known all his life about her athletic career, finally realized how important she was.

About this time, Steve Sulley, a lifelong baseball enthusiast living in neighboring Belleville, Illinois, was destined to become part of Erma's life. Without Erma knowing it, an entourage began to form around her, and Steve was a charter member.

His initial interest was the Negro leagues, introduced to him by Brenda, his wife of more than thirty-five years. She was in San Antonio visiting Steve's parents, and she came across an exhibit of memorabilia from the Negro leagues at the air force base. Steve's father spent thirty years in the U.S. Air Force, and Steve followed in his father's footsteps.

When the memorabilia came to Scott Air Force Base, Brenda encouraged Steve to see it. He got interested in the Negro leagues and learned there were three women players in the history of the league. One was a pitcher. Her name was Mamie Johnson, and she lived in Washington, D.C. While Steve was in our nation's capital on business, he called on Johnson and presented her with a jersey sporting her name on the back and a collection of articles that had been written about her. She told him she had applied to play in the AAGPBL but had been turned down. Only white women took the field in Erma's playing days.

Soon, Steve was investigating Erma's league. When he learned there were former players living in and around St. Louis, he immediately contacted them and invited them to brunch at Bevo Mill. That was the beginning of a close relationship that bound Erma and Steve together.

For the past ten years, Steve has been Erma's promoter, arranging autograph-signing events and speaking appearances.

Erma needed no promoter when the St. Louis Softball Hall of Fame selection committee in 1996 voted to induct her into their group of best local softball players, both men and women. She was fourteen years old in 1938 when she joined the Amateur Softball League. She played eight seasons at third base and outfield at the old St. Louis Softball Park at Shenandoah and Ohio Streets in South St. Louis. She played for Melber Bakery, Breimeyer Soda and Weick Funeral Home. In 1944, she was selected as an All-Star.

In 1996, Erma was inducted into the St. Louis Softball Hall of Fame. *Courtesy Erma Bergmann.*

Erma's two brothers and nephews got dressed up and attended the thirty-dollar-a-plate induction dinner at The Cedars, the popular banquet hall connected to St. Raymond's Maronite Catholic Church. Joe Phelan of the St. Louis Metropolitan Police Department introduced Erma. He ended by saying: "Erma is a true competitor, on the field, in the police department, and in life. Erma, you will always be a winner."

"It was a thrill going back to my roots where it all started," Erma remembered. Dave Sinclair of automotive success sponsored Erma. "I knew you were a policewoman, but I didn't know you had all those other credentials," Dave told Erma after the dinner.

When the calendar turned to the new century, Erma decided to add another important credential to her list. She officially joined the Catholic Church. She had deferred this decision for years. "What if I got married to somebody of a different religion? Which church would our kids go to?" She refused to subject her children to the same conflict she had endured as a youngster, torn between her father's Lutheran heritage and her mother's Catholic devotion. As she approached her seventy-sixth birthday, it seemed that marriage and children had eluded her and she could dismiss that worry.

Erma's family attended the thirty-dollar-a-plate induction dinner: nephew Johnny (*left*), nephew Victor (*right*) and brother Victor (*seated*). *Courtesy Erma Bergmann.*

She asked Rosemary Lyons, her former softball friend, to sponsor her for becoming a member of the Catholic Church. Years later, when Rosemary became ill, Erma visited her at Delmar Gardens nursing home. Erma told her friend: "You were a good woman. You were a good wife, you were a good mother." Tears welled up in both women's eyes. Erma believed in letting people know how she felt while they were alive.

"It doesn't do any good after they're dead," she reasoned. When Rosemary died, Erma sent a dozen red roses to the funeral home. "I want the biggest roses you have," she instructed the florist.

A few years later, Erma attended the 2008 St. Louis Softball Hall of Fame induction dinner, congratulating the younger softball players while she watched a gentleman at the head table puff on a lit cigar, caressing it with his lips and spinning it around in his mouth.

Erma sported a tiny baseball, glove and bat hanging from a chain around her neck, a gift from Julie Kurz, her closest friend.

Erma met Julie in the year 2000 in Dillard's department store's sportswear department. Julie is an elementary school teacher who spent that summer working in retail, saving money for a trip to Bolivia and Peru. One of Erma's hobbies, along with bowling and bingo, was shopping. So she and Julie got together often and became close friends.

The twosome traveled to Philadelphia to visit Erma's cousin. When Erma celebrated her eightieth birthday in 2004, she invited Julie to accompany her on a Celebrity cruise to Alaska.

One of the many people Julie and Erma met on the trip was Ariana Kudlo, a nine-year-old from California traveling with her brother and parents. They

When Erma celebrated her eightieth birthday, she invited her best friend, Julie Kurz, to accompany her on a cruise to Alaska. This picture was taken on the Celebrity cruise ship. *Courtesy Julie Kurz.*

spent a half day together riding on a bus through the rain forests of Alaska. The Kudlo family sent flowers to Erma's stateroom for her birthday, and Erma and Ariana wrote to each other.

"Erma tells me about signing autographs and being in the Hall of Fame. My letters aren't nearly as exciting as hers," Ariana said four years after the trip, when she became a teenager.

Erma and Julie extended their trip a few days when the cruise ship docked. Erma was unofficially adopted by Julie's family and was included in holiday celebrations as well as showers, weddings and graduations of Julie's twelve nieces and nephews.

Julie and her mother, Pat, joined Steve as members of Erma's entourage, traveling with her and former player Audrey to reunions and card shows.

This group, plus brother Otto and nephew Victor, also drove to Springfield, Missouri, for Erma's induction into the Missouri Sports Hall of Fame. Combined with the Softball Hall of Fame and the Baseball Hall of Fame in Cooperstown, this honor gave Erma a triple crown.

Erma M. "Bergie" Bergmann was the only woman among fifteen Missouri athletes to be enshrined in the 2007 class. By this time in her life, Bergie was accustomed to being outnumbered by men when she ventured into male territory.

Outnumbered she may be, but never intimidated. Today, she joins some three hundred athletes who have gone before her in the state's hall of fame. Names like Satchel Paige, Casey Stengel, Dizzy Dean and Bob Gibson are heard in the same breath as Erma's.

Hundreds of sports enthusiasts gathered at the Sports Hall of Fame on East Stan Musial Drive in Springfield to celebrate the class of 2007. The fans could shake hands with the athletes, secure their autographs and enjoy the exhibits in the handsome modern building, of which our state can be proud.

The Hall of Fame was built in 1994 by John Q. Hammons, the hotel developer and philanthropist who practically rebuilt Springfield. He also erected the eight-thousand-seat baseball stadium in Springfield to lure the St. Louis Cardinals' Class AA affiliate team to town.

An early evening media get-together saw Erma interviewed by Dan Gray of television's Fox 2 and featured in a few radio interviews to be aired throughout the state. Erma's rhinestone necklace and earrings, gifts from her deceased brother, sparkled against her long dark dress. Her white hair was beautifully coiffed, her makeup carefully applied. She looked like a movie star, the only feminine face in the inductees' official photograph.

About 1,600 people gathered in the University Plaza Convention Center for the evening banquet. The athletes made their way into the ballroom and seated themselves at the raised head table. Ozzie Smith climbed up to the head table and greeted Erma with a peck on the cheek before seating himself with her other guests. Ozzie had recommended Erma for inclusion in the Hall of Fame.

Above: Erma joined the Missouri Sports Hall of Fame at its home in Springfield. She was the only woman among fifteen athletes in the 2007 class. *Courtesy Gene Donaldson*.

Left: Erma looked her best at the installation dinner and gave a stirring speech. *Courtesy Gene Donaldson*.

The inductees signed autographs in the lobby after the dinner. *Courtesy Gene Donaldson.*

When it was her turn for comments, Erma spoke in a clear, strong voice, her words reaching all corners of the huge ballroom. She talked about her rise through athletics and her police career. She closed her remarks with, "I want to thank everyone here and not here for making this possible."

Erma's reaction to compliments on her remarks was: "I just tell it like it was. I don't flower it up. I just ad lib. When it's over, I don't even know what I said."

Folks gathered in the hotel lobby where refreshments and autographs were available. The owner of Sportsman's Park, a sports bar in Ladue, requested Erma's autograph and invited her and her entourage for lunch when they returned to St. Louis. Her group took advantage of his generous invitation a couple of months later.

Mayor Francis G. Slay declared February 11, 2007, the date of her induction, "Erma M. Bergmann Day" and issued the following declaration:

> *WHEREAS Erma M. Bergmann began playing amateur softball as a 14-year-old playing in the adult women's league, where her peers were 19 to 25 years old and was nicknamed "the kid;" and*
>
> *WHEREAS Erma played amateur softball for eight years until a professional scout selected her for a tryout at spring training. At the end of spring training, Max Carey commented that Erma was one of the best rookies in the 1946 spring training and selected her to play professional baseball; and*

A Springfield radio station interviewed Erma at the event. *Courtesy Gene Donaldson.*

WHEREAS Erma played professional baseball for six years for the All-American Girls Professional Baseball League and also played three years of professional baseball in the National Girls Baseball League with the Chicago Queens until girls professional baseball ended; and

WHEREAS Erma returned to St. Louis to attend the police academy, and she served her community honestly and honorably for 25 years until her retirement from the St. Louis Metropolitan Police Department; and

WHEREAS Erma has led her life as a model citizen and an ambassador in softball and baseball for generations to come. She is a role model for men, women, young adults and children alike, and truly deserves this induction into the Missouri Sports Hall of Fame. We join with her family, friends and former teammates in congratulating her on this prestigious honor.

Now therefore I, Francis G. Slay, Mayor of the City of St. Louis, do hereby proclaim February 11, 2007 as

"Erma M. Bergmann Day"
in the City of St. Louis

This handsomely framed proclamation hangs in Erma's home.

A fan from Hollister, Missouri, wrote Erma a note after the event:

I just want you to know I go to all of these inductions, but of all the people I have listened to, you were the most interesting. Also very kind and considerate of everyone around. I would like to ask you for an autograph for my granddaughter who is six. I want to share your story and the things you have accomplished in your life and let her know as a young lady she can do whatever she wants.

This letter writer called Erma and invited her to go to a Cardinals game with him and his wife. After the game, Erma took them to Hodak's, another one of her favorite restaurants. "Whoever would think that an old lady like me would be in three Halls of Fame," said the eighty-two-year-old baseball player. She was almost as pumped up as she was a half century ago, when she was a diva of the diamond.

Blessed with good health, Erma took no medicine and at this point in her life had no chronic health problems.

During an interview, the strains of "Take Me Out to the Ball Game" erupted from Erma's pocket, announcing a call on her cellphone. This call was an invitation to be part of FanFest 2009.

Baseball players and fans all agree, St. Louis is one of the best baseball towns in America. So, when it was announced that the 2009 All-Star Game would be played in St. Louis's Busch Stadium, the city burst with excitement. Banners decorated streetlights. Red, white and blue arches stretched across sidewalks. Park grounds downtown were decorated, as was the plaza around the stadium. The city prepared for FanFest 2009, a five-day baseball extravaganza that precedes every All-Star Game.

At the same time, Americans were enduring a two-year precipitous free fall in the economy. The plunge was compared to the Great Depression of the 1930s. The stock market lost more than one-third of its value, and unemployment soared to 10 percent. Some sixteen million Americans were looking for work, according to the U.S. Bureau of Labor Statistics. Doom and gloom hung over financial circles. But people who came to FanFest in 2009 could temporarily escape the black clouds that loomed overhead.

More than 150,000 people passed through the FanFest portal of America's Center, St. Louis's Convention and Visitors Center. Local fans and out-of-town enthusiasts shattered the previous year's attendance record. The turnout even topped the number of fans who attended the 2008 festivities in New York by 17 percent.

Fanatics, from which the word "fan" is derived, anteed up twenty-five dollars for kids and students and thirty dollars for adults. The fans could throw a pitch, run a base, smack a home run, see the memorabilia and displays and secure coveted autographs.

Baseball fans visiting the Sports Hall of Fame requested autographs. *Courtesy Gene Donaldson.*

Abraham Applegate of Centralia, Illinois, fired a forty-four-mile-an-hour pitch. This nine-year-old boy may have a pitching future. A 1993 Babe Ruth baseball card was going for more than $3,000. At the live auction, you could bid on a 1956 road jersey from Cardinals legend Stan Musial.

You could take home a first base bag that Albert Pujols had guarded at Busch Stadium if you had $150 to spend. Following tradition, Hall of Famer Ozzie Smith autographed a giant inflatable baseball during the opening ceremonies.

Fifty-two-year-old John Mohan of St. Louis County was one of the excited fans. One of his goals of attending FanFest was to get autographs from the female baseball players. "I have an eight-year-old daughter, and I want her to know that girls can do sports, too, not just boys. I want her to know that girls are as important as boys in sports," John explained. He worked at Ice & Fuel, a St. Louis sports bar and restaurant owned by his brother.

It all started when John bought a white baseball shirt with the All-American Girls Professional Baseball League logo at a fundraiser at a River City Rascals game. The Rascals is an independent professional men's baseball team that plays in the Frontier League at T.R. Hughes Ballpark in

O'Fallon, Missouri. John brought the shirt to FanFest and waited in line with thirty folks in front of him to meet the women from the league. "There were a hundred people in line when I left their table," John recalled.

John hit an autograph bonanza. Erma was flanked by Audrey Kissel Lafser, Erma's buddy and lead-off hitter who played second base for the Minneapolis Millerettes in 1944, and Barbara Hoffmann, who spent 1951 and 1952 with the South Bend Blue Sox. Barbara was selected for the 1952 All-Star team and hit a home run in the contest.

Delores "Dolly" Brumfield White of Arkadelphia, Arkansas, and Shirley "Hustle" Burkovich of Palm Springs, California, flew to St. Louis for FanFest. Dolly was only fourteen years old when she reported to Havana, Cuba, in 1947 for spring training in the women's baseball league. The scout came to her house in Mobile, Alabama, to get her mother's permission to allow her to play ball. The scout said, "I'll take her, and we'll let her play ball." Dolly's mother replied, "I don't want you to take her. I just want you to let her play."

Dolly led the Kenosha Comets in hitting in 1951 and finished second in the league in 1953. She became president of the All-American Girls Professional Baseball League Players' Association Inc. and is a regular at FanFests. "We're a part of history. We're role models for children," said the seventy-seven-year-old. "Less than 50 percent of us are still living. We lose an average of one former player a month." After her baseball career, Dolly earned three degrees, including a doctorate in education. She taught physical education for forty years.

One of Dolly's goals was to get women's baseball in the U.S. Olympics in 2016. Unfortunately, the Olympic Committee did not approve women's baseball. When the Little League for boys' baseball was formed, a case went to the U.S. Supreme Court to have the same privilege for girls, she remembered.

Baseball was one of seven sports competing for perhaps two slots at the Olympic Games in 2016, according to the Society for American Baseball Research. The International Baseball Federation's (IBF) campaign to grow women's baseball around the world sparked the proposal. Between three hundred thousand and five hundred thousand girls and women play baseball around the world, says the IBF.

"We're building bridges. That's the reason I have been coming to FanFest for ten years," Dolly added. "I give Mr. Wrigley credit for giving us women a chance, although he wouldn't approve of the way I look today. You could not have short hair and you couldn't appear in public in shorts or slacks when we were playing ball."

The late Shirley Burkovich toured with the 1950 Springfield Sallies and Chicago Colleens and played with Rockford in 1951. She hailed from Swissvale, Pennsylvania, near Pittsburgh, and moved to Palm Springs after she hung up her glove for the last time. She was treasurer of the players' association and had a speaking part in the movie *A League of Their Own*. She enjoyed the camaraderie at FanFests and the players' reunions. The first reunion was held in 1988, and Shirley had attended them all. They were held biennially until 2005, when the players decided to get together every year.

In addition to signing baseballs, bats, shirts and caps, the ladies autographed about three thousand sheets bearing copies of their baseball cards and playing statistics. Coordinators of the event printed the sheets for the ladies' signatures. Erma suffered shoulder discomfort in the evening following the day-long signings. The pitcher who had fired the ball so hard her catcher stuffed a piece of foam rubber inside her mitt to protect her hand now had an aching shoulder from wielding a pen.

Then the ladies moved to another part of the St. Louis Convention Center, where they seated themselves in chairs on a baseball diamond. Here they fielded questions from the audience sitting in the stands and from the moderator of the question-and-answer period. A question frequently asked was, "How much money did you make?" The ballplayers' salaries ranged from $45.00 to $85.00 a week during the first years of play to a peak of $125.00 a week in later years. Erma earned $75.00 a week plus a $3.50 daily meal allowance when the team was on the road. In 1951, playing in Battle Creek, Michigan, she was paid $85.00 a week. It was enough for her to buy a used black Chevrolet convertible with a white top and a red and gray interior. By this time, she was in Miami, and the white wall tires rolled to the beach every day.

The five days of FanFest were both exhausting and exhilarating for these former athletes now in their seventies and eighties.

What was even more high-spirited was the AAGPBL reunion in Milwaukee in September 2009. These athletes, now in the late innings of their lives, relished the memories of playing baseball in their prime. "You have to remember we ate together, we traveled on the bus together, we slept together and we played ball together. We were a family," Erma reminded me. The women relived their camaraderie and the good times they enjoyed when they were together. They all agreed that their ball-playing seasons were the best years of their lives.

About a dozen players congregated in the hotel bar for a nightcap or lively banter. Celeste Klause, then a senior at the University of Michigan near Grand Rapids, was majoring in film and video production. With her microphone and camera set up, she interviewed the players while they relaxed. Erma told the interviewer, "We put women's sports on the map after *A League of Their Own* was shown."

Dolly White said, "We could do things that women of that time couldn't do." They could travel and have dinner as a group at elegant restaurants unaccompanied by men. "The league influenced me to go to college because some girls were enrolled in college," she remembered. The video production documenting women's baseball history was scheduled to be sent to the Library of Congress.

As the college student studied these older women, it was remarkable to note how they had maintained their athletic figures. Erma's 150 pounds covered her five-foot, seven-inch frame, and she weighed just slightly less than she did when she fired the ball over the plate. Her former colleagues were also slim and trim, as if ready to trot out to their positions on the diamond. Weight-loss leaders would delight in knowing the secret to their success.

The hotel employee who drove the hostelry's van said, "Of all the groups we've had here [at the Clarion Hotel near the airport], this one has been the most fun." The driver picked the ladies up at the airport on Thursday and Friday and transported them to church on Sunday morning.

Sister Toni Palermo, a School Sister of St. Francis from the Rockford, Illinois province, shepherded Erma and the group out of the van and up the steps at St. Stephen's Catholic Church. She pulled on the railing, favoring a new knee that had replaced her arthritic one about six weeks prior to the reunion. She had been Concetta Palermo before she entered the convent. During her baseball years, she was nicknamed "Peanuts" and "Mighty Mouse" for her small stature and surprising strength. Peanuts was fourteen years old when she joined the ladies' baseball league and played shortstop.

The white-haired priest standing at the top of the steps greeting parishioners on their way into church asked about this group of ladies pouring from the hotel van like clowns spilling from a circus car. When he learned who they were, he excitedly welcomed them, pumping their hands as they entered church. He greeted them again from the altar, explaining their place in sports history to the congregation. Then he began the Mass.

Sister Toni hails from Chicago, where she competed in all available sports, as well as creative dance, in her school years. She learned to choreograph dance routines. Erma marveled at the athletic opportunities afforded Toni Palermo. "We only had volleyball and swimming for girls at McKinley High School," she bemoaned.

Scouts from the women's baseball league started noticing this natural athlete when she was eleven years old, but Toni put them off. "The scouts wanted me to go to Cuba for spring training," Sister Toni told the *Catholic Herald* staff in Madison, Wisconsin, during an interview. "I thought they were crazy. I didn't have any concept of how good I was."

She played two years of professional softball, then joined the league and played with the Chicago Colleens and the Springfield Sallies. It wasn't a glamorous life, according to this shortstop. "We'd play a night game, shower, get on the bus, go to the next town, get there at two or three in the morning," Sister Toni said. Then there were radio interviews and practice from 8:00 a.m. to noon. The players were free until 5:00 p.m., when it was time for more practice leading up to game time. "Not only were we not getting a lot of sleep, but we played our guts out to beat each other," the nun remembered.

It was in South Bend, Indiana, at spring training that God intervened in this shortstop's life. She had planned to enter the convent in September, but she decided to leave spring training and return home. She knew how deep and passionate her love of baseball was, and she was afraid if she played out the season, she would forgo becoming a nun.

So Sister Toni emerged from the baseball dugout for the last time, traded her uniform for the long brown habit of the Franciscans and entered the convent. She took her final vows more than six decades ago, a member of the class of 1954. As a Franciscan nun and now a licensed psychotherapist, she earned a bachelor's degree, three master's degrees and a doctorate and taught school. She attends most of the women's baseball reunions and is vice-president of the players' association.

Sister Toni found another home on the tennis court and played competitively in singles and doubles in the 1990s. Her serve has whizzed across the net in tennis tournaments in Florida, California, Texas and Arizona. She has also danced across the tennis court at the Marin Cricket Club in Philadelphia and played on regional teams. She formerly taught everything from folk to disco dancing.

"Weekend competitions are my therapy," she said during the Milwaukee reunion. In 1994, Sister Toni was added to the Wall of Fame in the Nielsen

Tennis Stadium in Madison, Wisconsin, where she now lives. She spends her retirement years teaching disadvantaged people how to manage money and helps them find jobs. She also assists senior citizens in her parish.

Fifty-two former players traveled to Milwaukee by plane or car for the September 2009 reunion. Since Erma played six years in the league, many of the women at the reunion either played with her or against her. Name tags refreshed memories, as half a century alters a woman's appearance. Most of the attendees remembered Erma and greeted her warmly. Erma returned their embraces.

When Erma spied Sophie Kurys, the two players wrapped their arms around each other. A flood of emotions filled their faces. "Hi, Polsky," Erma said, calling Sophie by the nickname Erma gave her. It refers to Sophie's Polish descent. Sophie was a Racine Belle from 1943 to 1951, and Erma played with her for two of those seasons. She averaged 150 stolen bases per season, with a career high of 201 in 1946. She reached base 215 times that year and stole 201 bases in 203 attempts. It was quite a feat to be thrown out only 2 times out of more than 200 tries. She set a world record with 1,114 career stolen bases. That's more than Ty Cobb's 892 and better than Lou Brock's 938 career steals. Sophie's 201 stolen bases in a single season still stands as a professional record. *Newsweek* in

This oral history interview was recorded by a University of Michigan student in 2009 during the All-American Girls Professional Baseball Players reunion in Milwaukee. The author (*right*) observes the interview. *Courtesy Gene Donaldson.*

1946 called Sophie the "speedy second baseman" and the "Tina Cobb" of the league.

The base stealer traveled from her home in Scottsdale, Arizona, to see her former friends from the diamond. Sophie and Erma's pleasure in seeing each other made the trip worthwhile for both of them. Little did Erma know that this would be the last time she would see Sophie. The renowned base stealer and Player of the Year in 1946 passed away in February 2013, making national sports news.

"Take Me Out to the Ball Game" bellowed from Erma's cellphone tucked in her heavy purse. Her nephew was calling to tell her that Dave Sinclair, a longtime friend in St. Louis, had died of gallbladder cancer at age eighty-one. An aura of sadness temporarily clouded Erma's weekend.

Sinclair was a highly respected man in the St. Louis community. After serving in World War II in the U.S. Army, he came home and became a hod carrier, hauling heavy, wet plaster up ladders at construction sites. He then joined the St. Louis Police Department like his father and grandfather. After five years, he traded in his blue police officer's uniform for a car salesman's coat and tie in the hopes of making more money to support his growing family.

He was so successful that Ford Motor Company set him up with his own dealership. This was the beginning of his automobile dynasty of four dealerships. Along the way, he never turned down an opportunity to help someone, including Erma. When the female baseball players celebrated their sixtieth anniversary reunion at Baseball's Hall of Fame, Dave Sinclair lent Erma a van to drive to Cooperstown, New York, for the event.

"For me, Dave?" she queried. "Yes, for you, Erma," Dave replied. "I'll never forget Dave Sinclair for that as long as I know who I am," Erma said. Her regret was that she wasn't in St. Louis to attend his funeral and express her appreciation to his family of seven children, thirty-seven grandchildren and one great-granddaughter.

Dave Sinclair's advertising car slogan was, "If it's not right, we'll make it right." He made a lot of things right for a lot of people during his lifetime. It is estimated that there were five hundred cars in his funeral procession. Many of the vehicles were probably bought from Sinclair salesmen. Erma's old Dodge van would have been in the line if she had been home. Erma tucked her sadness in her heart and returned to the reunion.

Isabel "Lefty" Alvarez, seventy-six years old with cropped white hair and cheeks flushed with excitement, remembered growing up in Havana, Cuba. "My mother had a vision for me," she said in slightly broken

English. When the women's teams came to Cuba for spring training in 1947, her mother seized the opportunity for Isabel to escape Havana's squalor. She arranged for her daughter to join the league at fourteen years of age. Lefty later played first base for six years, touring with the Chicago Colleens, then joining the Fort Wayne team. Several Cuban girls became AAGPBL players.

Lefty stayed in the United States when she retired from playing ball, worked in factories and often visiting her family in Havana. She arrived at the Milwaukee reunion behind the wheel of her 1994 Chrysler convertible.

The reunion's theme, "Power of the Human Spirit," seemed to embody the physical, mental and emotional fervor of these former ball players. The theme played out at Saturday's luncheon, when honored legends in the world of women's sports joined their counterparts. An autograph session preceded the legends' luncheon at Milwaukee's Italian Community Center.

Billie Jean King was one of those legends. In 1973, she defeated Bobby Riggs, a former Wimbledon men's tennis champion, in "The Battle of the Sexes." The match was significant, because it garnered greater recognition and respect for women's tennis. King said at the time: "I thought it would set us back fifty years if I didn't win that match. It would have ruined the women's [tennis] tour and would have affected all women's self-esteem."

Billie Jean was one of the featured speakers at the luncheon. She addressed the women ballplayers as "sheroes" instead of heroes. "We all stand on your shoulders," she told them. "Without you, there wouldn't be us."

Billie Jean King won twelve Grand Slam singles titles, sixteen Grand Slam women's doubles titles and eleven Grand Slam mixed doubles titles. In 2009, President Barack Obama awarded her the Presidential Medal of Freedom. She founded the Women's Tennis Association, the Women's Sports Foundation and World Team Tennis. Some guests at the Legends luncheon brought tennis racquets for her to sign.

King's prowess didn't end on the tennis court. She has spent her adult life fighting for equal rights for women in sports and in all walks of life. In the late 1960s, she lobbied for equal prize money in the men's and women's tennis games. By 1973, the U.S. Open had become the first major tournament to pay equal prize money for men and women. Her goal was accomplished.

In 2010 at the Australian Open, Serena Williams tied Billie Jean's record. Williams's victory over Justine Henin in women's singles gave her twelve Grand Slam singles titles. Williams said to an Associated Press reporter: "To tie Billie Jean King is cool. But, honestly, my whole thing is to do what she did off the court."

"When I think of Billie Jean King, I don't even think about tennis. I think about all the amazing things that she's done. And that's what I want to do, with every aspect of my life," confided Serena Williams.

"Never underestimate the human spirit," Billie Jean admonished the crowd from the speaker's stand. Then she acknowledged the other legends present.

The first living legend was Ria Cortesio, one of few female umpires in professional baseball. She umpired a spring training game between the Chicago Cubs and the Arizona Diamondbacks.

Elaine Gonya played in the first women's professional football league in Wisconsin. She was a defensive back and led the league in interceptions two consecutive seasons. She was a member of the bronze medal United States North Team Handball Team in the U.S. Olympic Festival in 1994. Elaine has completed ten marathons, including the Boston, Chicago and U.S. Marine Corps races.

Dawn Riley is one of the best-known sailors in the world. She was the first woman to manage an entire America's Cup syndicate. She was the first American to sail in three America's Cups and two Whitbread Round the World races.

Julienne Simpson played basketball and was named All-American four times between 1971 and 1975. In 1975, she played for the U.S. team, which won a gold medal at the PanAmerican Games. In 1976, she made the Olympic team. She later became a women's college basketball coach at Arizona State University.

These legends, who raised the bar, joined their forerunners from the baseball diamond. Ninety-one-year-old Mary Pratt, who pitched for four years for the Kenosha Comets and the Rockford Peaches, was the matriarch of the legends. Sophie Kurys held base-stealing honors. She hailed from Flint, Michigan, and was dubbed the "Flint Flash." She was voted Player of the Year in 1947.

Lou Arnold of Pawtucket, Rhode Island, rolled around the reunion, seated in her walker. She joined Jean Cione, a left-handed pitcher and first baseman from 1945 to 1954; Audrey Haines Daniels originally from Winnipeg, Manitoba; and Katie Horstman, a catcher, infielder and pitcher from Minster, Ohio.

Both groups of legends recognized the other's accomplishments and appreciated their impact in the world of women's sports. They were perfect matches.

Back at the hotel, the players autographed bats that were auctioned at charity events throughout the year and throughout the country.

School buses rolled up to the hotel on Sunday afternoon and drove the players to Miller Park for a Milwaukee Brewers game. Before they entered the ballpark, the ladies lined up outside the stadium and posed for pictures. They burst into song with a rousing rendition of their victory anthem, an emotional moment for singers and listeners alike. Happily, they then stepped inside the stadium.

On the way to their seats, they stopped to study the window display of All-American Girls Professional Baseball League memorabilia. Tears came to some eyes as they relived the memories conjured up by seeing the uniform, cap, balls and photos of their heyday.

After the game, the closing banquet featured another winner, Mary Wallace "Wally" Funk. Wally was one of Mercury 13, a group of thirteen women pilots who secretly tested to become America's first woman in space. Wally was twenty-one years old when she applied for the program. The New Mexico native was a flight instructor at Fort Sill, Oklahoma. She earned a university degree from Oklahoma State, collegiate flight team awards and three thousand flying hours, an extraordinary number for someone so young.

Now, forty-eight years later, Wally stood before this audience of fellow high achievers. She's tall and thin and warm and friendly. Her thick, short, white hair was brushed back. She wore a dark suit, similar to a flight instructor's uniform, complete with white shirt and tie.

She described the rigorous testing she endured during the space program. It included pouring ice water in her ears and being twirled around on a machine to test for vertigo. She spent ten hours and thirty minutes in sensory isolation and did not utter a single word. And she gave no evidence of having reached the limit of her tolerance.

Wally passed the tests with flying colors, but the program was scrapped by Vice President Lyndon Johnson, who scrawled "Let's Stop This Now!" across the proposal to consider female astronauts. More than twenty years passed before Sally Ride's historic space flight in 1983.

Wally has been a professional pilot since 1957 and has accumulated more than seventeen thousand hours of flying time. The Smithsonian National Air and Space Museum asked her to speak about her life in its IMAX Theater. In 1964, she was the youngest woman in the history of Stephen's College to receive the Alumna Achievement Award, for her work in aviation.

In 1995, Wally joined seven of the Mercury 13 as guests of Lieutenant Colonel Eileen Collins, when she became the first female to pilot a space shuttle.

And she wasn't finished yet. At age seventy-five, she applied to be a passenger aboard Virgin Galactic's first space plane flight, which was scheduled for 2014. This flight never took off.

"I'll be flying 'til I die," Wally said.

Wally's parents always told her, "Follow your dreams." As with the professional female baseball players in the audience, some dreams know no limits. And some ambitions are as lofty as Wally's desire to travel to the moon.

Erma's reunion ended on this high note, and the baseball players vowed to see one another in 2010 in Detroit for the next get together.

But Erma's brother's illness and death that year preempted her attending the 2010 baseball reunion.

14

BLAZING NEW TRAILS

Time does a number on everyone.
—Erma Bergmann

T ake Me Out to the Ball Game" pealed from Erma's cellphone on
Thanksgiving morning in 2010. The call was from the nursing home
where Erma's brother had spent the last six months of his life, battling
cancer. He succumbed to the disease that Thanksgiving Day. Erma's face
wrinkled in grief, and tears clouded her eyes while she spoke to the caller
from the nursing home.

"I'm all alone now," she cried, thinking of her brother, with whom she had
lived for the past eighty-five years. A monumental adjustment awaited Erma.

Tests had been performed in mid-May to determine Otto's illness and
method of treatment, but on May 24, he fell in the kitchen and broke his
hip. Erma lifted the six-foot, two-inch man and set him on a kitchen chair.
Then she called 911.

The paramedics took him to the hospital, and he had surgery on his hip.
He withstood the surgery well and entered a nursing home for rehabilitation
to walk again. Then he was diagnosed with cancer of the pancreas, lymph
nodes and prostate gland. His doctor told Erma and her nephew Victor that
Otto's cancer was aggressive and that Otto did not have long to live. Otto
discontinued the hip rehabilitation and lived the rest of his life in bed or in a
wheelchair in the nursing home.

Erma visited him almost every day, driving thirty miles round trip to see her brother. She usually pushed his wheelchair to an atrium area, where entertainment lightened their loads. With her usual friendly demeanor, "Bergie" got to know the employees and delighted in distributing her baseball cards.

On the day Otto died, Erma was scheduled to have Thanksgiving dinner with her friend Julie and her family. She proceeded with her plans and later spent the night at Julie's house.

Her friends rallied around to support Erma during this trying time. Steve Sulley, her self-appointed manager, drove from Belleville, Illinois, to console Erma. We raised our beer glasses and toasted Otto at the Haven, a pub a few doors from Erma's house. Beer was Otto's preferred beverage. Erma was happily handing out her signed baseball cards to waitresses and customers, but when she thought about Otto, her mood blackened, like a heavy drape blocking the light. Erma spent the nights at Julie's house from the time Otto died until his funeral.

Visitation was held at Kutis Funeral Home. Tom Kutis's father, from whom young Tom had taken over the business, had crossed Erma's path many years earlier, during her softball career. At that time, Mr. Kutis told her he wished she had played softball for his establishment instead of for a competitor. Erma said she would have been glad to play for him if he had asked her.

Erma received visitors at the funeral home. She was an attractive eighty-six-year-old. A black V-neck dress and three-quarter-length sleeves covered her slender body. She had lost a few pounds during Otto's illness. Stylish Cuban heels replaced her tennis shoes. She clutched a handful of signed baseball cards should someone come in who didn't already have her trademark. She laughed heartily when someone joked about her bringing her cards.

She greeted Bill, who lives across the street, and Freddie, a childhood friend who drove from Jefferson City to pay his respects. Both men had visited Otto during his illness.

Reverend Jason Rust, a pastor from Trinity Lutheran Church, where Otto, Victor and Erma had been baptized and confirmed many years earlier, officiated at Otto's funeral. As a veteran, Otto was buried in Jefferson Barracks National Cemetery with military honors. Shots fired by the honor guard pierced the air, and the bugle mourned "Taps." Marines in full dress uniform removed the flag from the casket, ceremoniously folded it and presented it to Erma, along with the casings of the spent rifle shells. She took the casings home and placed them with the casing from the police bullet she had fired at the burglar jumping the fence many years before.

Erma treated the family and a few friends to lunch at Garavelli's Cafeteria, where Erma and Otto often ate. Otto would have been pleased with his send-off.

Then she began the arduous task of reclaiming her life and coming to terms with the fact that she, the oldest of the family, was the only one left. She called on her herculean inner strength, surrounded herself with people—including strangers in a shopping mall—and began living the rest of her life.

Her spirits lifted when Eldon Arteaga suggested she apply for the George Washington Honor Medal awarded by the St. Louis Chapter of the Freedoms Foundation at Valley Forge. The annual awards recognize Americans whose positive words and deeds promote our country's rich heritage and unique freedoms.

Eldon Arteaga's path had crossed Erma's many times through the years, with his face pressed against a camera. Arteaga Photography was founded by Eldon's father, and the company is a premier St. Louis photography studio. When Erma was on the business end of Mr. Arteaga's lens, she was often in action, perhaps throwing out the first pitch when the U.S. Olympic softball team passed through St. Louis for an exhibition game.

Or she may have been tossing the first pitch at Lafayette Park for the St. Louis Perfectos, the vintage baseball club that plays by 1860 rules.

Or she may have been sitting on the stage at the Missouri Historical Society with Audrey Kissel Lafser and Barbara Hoffmann, answering questions after the viewing of *A League of Their Own*. The occasion was the traveling exhibit from Cooperstown. Visitors to the museum stood in line for almost two hours to meet the female professional baseball players portrayed in the movie and to secure their autographs.

In 2005, these three ballplayers were guests of the St. Louis University girls' basketball team and honored with a plaque from the university athletic director, Cheri Levick, on National Girls and Women's Sports Day. "These pioneers of women's sports contributed and paved the way for young women to excel in university and professional sports," said Levick at the award presentation.

Two years later, this baseball threesome was invited to participate in the Shades of Green Jamboree for the Girl Scouts of Eastern Missouri. The event, held in December 2007 at America's Center, St. Louis's convention center, celebrated ninety-five years of scouting. Erma and her player friends

Some 1,700 Girl Scouts attended the Shades of Green Jamboree at America's Center in St. Louis in celebration of ninety-five years of scouting. Erma, Audrey Lafser and Barbara Hoffman signed their baseball cards. *Courtesy Gene Donaldson.*

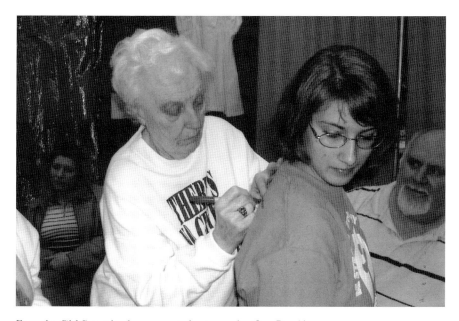

Even the Girl Scout leaders requested autographs. *Gene Donaldson.*

greeted and signed autographs for many of the 1,700 Girl Scouts who enjoyed the jamboree. Even the scout leaders lined up to have the women ballplayers sign the backs of their green T-shirts.

One scout leader announced, "I'll never wash this shirt." It was a great day for women in sports, as the St. Louis trio encouraged the scouts to pursue their goals and dreams.

Eldon Arteaga said: "Erma's a powerhouse. She did things that the average woman was afraid to do back then."

This comment came from the man who stood almost six hundred feet in the air on top of the Gateway Arch snapping pictures as the second-to-last piece was slipped into place. His father took Eldon's picture from a helicopter. St. Louis's monument signifying the Gateway to the West was completed on October 28, 1965, 988 days after it was begun. Arteaga Photography was hired to take pictures once a month to document the building progress for Macdonald Construction Company, the principal contractor. The firm took twelve thousand pictures of the arch.

James Murphy, sheriff of St. Louis, wrote a letter recommending Erma for the George Washington Honor Medal. He mentioned her twenty-five years of distinguished service as one of the first commissioned female officers in the St. Louis Metropolitan Police Department. He called her an outstanding role model exemplifying good citizenship and high moral character.

When the medal was awarded to Erma at a luncheon, Eldon was there to record the event with his camera.

It was early in 2006 when Otto and Erma had breakfast at a McDonald's and a customer walked up to her and said, "You're Erma the ballplayer, aren't you?" She didn't know him and never learned how he knew her.

It was the same year that Erma strolled into the state license bureau to renew her driver's license. Much to her dismay, she failed the eye test. "Here I was a good athlete and a sharpshooter in the police department and I can't even pass the eye test," Erma bemoaned. A trip to an ophthalmologist determined that macular degeneration was the culprit, and Erma was referred to Levent Akduman, MD, a retina specialist.

Erma was eighty-one years old when she was diagnosed. Macular degeneration is an age-related disease. About 10 percent of people over the age of seventy-five develop the disease, according to Erma's doctor. Dr. Akduman is a native of Turkey and studied medicine at Hacettepe University in Ankara. He came to St. Louis in 1993 for a fellowship at Washington University School of Medicine. He followed that with a fellowship at the Barnes Retina Institute ending in 1996. He then became an instructor in

Washington University School of Medicine's Ophthalmology Department. In 2001, he was appointed an associate professor at Saint Louis University Eye Institute, where Erma saw him on a regular basis.

He explained that macular degeneration has two forms, dry and wet. The dry form, accounting for 80 percent of cases, causes yellow deposits in the retina, but a person usually doesn't notice it. As the disease progresses, 10 percent of patients with the dry condition convert to wet. The wet form is so named because abnormal blood vessels leak fluid or blood into and under the macula. The transformation from dry to wet is responsible for the most profound vision loss if not promptly treated. According to Dr. Akduman, it is the most common cause of elderly legal blindness, which is vision worse than 20/200 in the better-sighted eye.

Dr. Akduman ordered a fluorescein angiography, photographs of the retina used for diagnosis. In Erma's case, she was diagnosed with the wet form in her right eye and the dry form in her left eye. At the time she failed the eye test to renew her driver's license, her vision had slipped suddenly to 20/300 in her right eye. Her sight had been in the 20/30 range for years, but almost overnight her vision rapidly deteriorated. It was no wonder panic gripped Erma.

Some years before, Erma had had cataracts removed from both eyes. Lens implants enabled her to read with one eye and see at a distance with the other eye. It was the distance eye that was affected by this disease threatening her ability to drive. So she mustered her strength to see what had to be done to save her sight. She might have had the same feeling when she was perched on the top of the pitching mound with the bases loaded and nobody out in a tied game.

Erma didn't realize it at that time, but she was on the cusp of blazing another trail. Dr. Akduman explained to her that medicine injected into the eye was new and was the only treatment available. The prescription medicine, Lucentis, had been developed by Genetech Inc. of South San Francisco, California. Dawn Kelmar of Genetech said Lucentis had been in development and trial stages for about ten years. Retina specialists across the country were delighted that something was on the market to help their patients. Dr. Akduman received his first shipment of Lucentis on July 10, 2006, but the medicine was so new that it had not yet been approved by Medicare. Erma's first injection was postponed until July 21, when Medicare would cover the cost.

Her friend Julie accompanied her to the doctor's office. With her head held high and her back straight and tall, Erma marched into the office, steps ahead of Julie, and climbed into the chair. Dr. Akduman gently lowered the back so she was lying flat. Numbing drops were inserted into her eye, and Dr. Akduman administered the injection. Erma didn't flinch. The procedure took only seconds and was painless. She felt a slight pressure in her eye but no pain. She left the office, her eye uncovered, relieved that it was over. On her way out, Erma smiled broadly and handed the office girls her autographed baseball card. She and Julie stopped at a Chinese restaurant for dinner on the way home. "It didn't hurt at all the next day," Erma remarked.

A couple of weeks later, Erma sat in a booth at Steak 'n Shake downing two cups of regular coffee at 10:00 p.m., and said "I think my vision is slightly better."

Dr. Akduman evaluated the historic injection for his patient. "It's unbelievable. It's like a miracle," he said. He wrote a letter to the license bureau stating it was safe for her to drive during the day. She took the eye test again; this time, she passed. She was issued her driver's license with no restriction.

The St. Louis Cardinals honored the three local AAGPBL players at Busch Stadium in 2003. Steve Sulley, friend of the players, stands behind them in the middle photo. *Courtesy Erma Bergmann.*

Her condition required almost twenty injections over a period of a few years to maintain her improved vision.

In 2013, another setback shook her emotional timbers. Dr. Akduman informed Erma that the dry condition in her left eye had worsened to wet degeneration, requiring injections in that eye, too. At age eighty-eight, Erma saw her eye doctor every few months. But she continued to drive her van, adding to its 120,000 miles.

Dr. Akduman said: "Erma was one of the lucky patients who received this treatment promptly, and she responded very favorably. She always kept a positive attitude."

Erma's doctor was so proud of his star patient that he profiled her and her successful treatment to about one thousand internationally recognized retina specialists at the Mediterranean Retina Meeting in Istanbul in 2008. The next year, he made the same presentation to almost ten thousand ophthalmologists and researchers at the Association for Research in Vision and Ophthalmology meeting in Fort Lauderdale, Florida.

Erma seemed destined to make history, and 2011 turned out to be a banner year. She was inducted into the St. Louis Sports Hall of Fame, the only woman among twelve honorees. St. Louis celebrated its lifelong citizen, its outstanding athlete and its law enforcement pioneer at a dinner in the ballroom of the Millennium Hotel.

Greg Marecek, founder and president of the Hall of Fame, introduced Erma, who sat on stage with the other honorees. He praised her accomplishments and added, "Her handwriting is remarkable." Even as she approached her ninetieth birthday, her script flowed easily and legibly.

Erma approached the microphone, her eyes scanning the eight hundred faces turned to her and waiting for her remarks. "You never know what you can do if you don't try," she told the audience. "My life would never have been as glamorous or as amorous as it was without baseball," she said with a smile gliding across her face.

Tim Moore, operations director for the Hall of Fame, later said, "Character is an important part of what a role model is, and we want to honor good individuals who represent the good part of the community." Erma fit the bill to a tee.

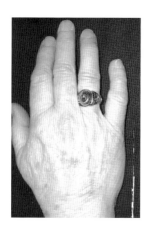

Erma liked to show her ring from the Baseball Hall of Fame in Cooperstown, New York. *Courtesy Gene Donaldson.*

Missouri Life, a statewide magazine, listed Erma among the state's fifty all-time sports heroes in its August 2011 issue. Bergie keeps good company with the likes of Dizzy Dean, Lou Brock and Yogi Berra in the baseball corner of the St. Louis Sports Hall of Fame.

Erma began to spend more time at home, cooking beef stew or Polish sausage, mashed potatoes and sauerkraut. Limburger cheese spread on Jewish rye bread was one of her favorite meals.

Life slowed some for Erma, but when she did make an appearance, she was still treated like a celebrity. She and a few other inductees attended a membership party for the St. Louis Sports Hall of Fame at a sports bar. When she was introduced, she stood, and men at the party lined up to meet her. She greeted them with a glowing smile and handed them her signed baseball cards, now coveted memorabilia of a professional baseball player.

She was invited to the sixtieth anniversary of the departure of the American League's Browns to Baltimore to become the Orioles. The luncheon was given by the St. Louis Browns Historical Society at the Sheraton Chalet in Westport in St. Louis County. Don Larsen, who in 1956 pitched the only perfect game in World Series history, was the speaker. Erma was the headliner of special guests and was introduced to the crowd of almost three hundred baseball fans. After the event, men clustered around Erma's table, shaking her hand and asking for her autograph. You'd think she was a movie star!

But when the All-American Girls Professional Baseball League celebrated its seventieth anniversary in the fall of 2013 in Chicago, Erma decided to stay home. "Most of the girls I played with are dead," she said, faced with the reality of outliving many of her peers. Although her entourage encouraged her to go and would have been happy to accompany her, "What fun would it be if I didn't know anybody," was her final answer. It was never easy to change Erma's mind.

When Erma thought about her ninety years of life, she said, "I've been blessed with good parents, good health and good athletic ability. Like Frank Sinatra sings, 'I've done it my way.'"

Opposite: The All-American Girls Professional Baseball League acknowledged Erma's baseball career when she died in September 2015. *Courtesy of the All-American Girls Professional Baseball League.*